Together in Rhythm

A Facilitator's Guide to **Drum Circle Music**

D1441026

Kalani

Alfred Publishing Co., Inc.
Los Angeles

Alfred Publishing Co., Inc.
Alfred.com

ISBN 0-7390-3509-6 (Book)

ISBN 0-7390-3510-X (Book and DVD)

Library of Congress Cataloging-in-Publication Data

Kalani.

Together in rhythm : a facilitator's guide to drum circle music / Kalani.

p. cm.

Includes bibliographical references (p. 102).

ISBN 0-7390-3509-6 (pbk.) -- ISBN 0-7390-3510-X (pbk. with DVD)

1.   Drum circles--Instruction and study. I. Title.

MT736.K35 2004

786.9'071--dc22

2004013016

About the Author

Kalani is one of the world's foremost drum circle facilitators, a keynote presenter, trainer, accomplished studio and touring percussionist, world-music composer, educator, and award-winning author. His personable, down-to-earth style inspires participants to celebrate life though music and helps them to develop better relationships with their fellow students, co-workers, families and friends.

Kalani has received numerous awards for his work as a drum circle facilitator, percussion clinician, performer and author. He presents workshops and seminars for the International Music Products Association (NAMM), the Percussive Arts Society, the National Association of Music Educators (MENC), the American Orff-Schulwerk Association, the American Music Therapy Association, the American Music Conference, the Los Angeles Philharmonic, the National Academy of Recording Arts and Sciences (the Grammy Foundation), and numerous other state and regional music education organizations.

He is the founder and director of Programs for Rhythm Gym, a 501(c)3 non-profit organization dedicated to promoting health and active music making (Rhythmgym.org). He is the artistic director of World Rhythms drum and dance programs, which preserve and promote music, dance and cross-cultural appreciation through educational resources and experiences (DrumCamp.com).

Kalani is a featured musician on recordings from Disney, Warner Brothers, Tri-Star, Paramount, the Nature Company, and Jim Hensen Records. He has performed and recorded with such music legends as Kenny Loggins, David Sanborn, Max Roach, Barry Manilow, Vic Damone, John Mayall, Chante Moore, Dr. John, Suzanne Ciani, and Melissa Manchester, and he is the featured percussionist on the *Yanni: Live at the Acropolis video and CD*. He has released two CDs of original music, *Pangea* and *Insights*, and has produced a number of instructional books and DVDs.

Kalani is an intuitive musical coach who helps people from all walks of life to learn, work, and live together in rhythm. He works closely with several of the music industry's top companies as an instrument and program design consultant. A certified Orff-Schulwerk educator, he travels throughout the world as a drum circle facilitator, music educator, performer, presenter and trainer, and his programs are well-represented in music stores and educational institutions. He is a pioneer in the field of combining music and wellness, and has developed strategies that are used in health clubs and schools to promote community-healthy choices and life skills.

Kalani's primary sponsors include Toca Percussion instruments, Gibraltar hardware, Paiste cymbals, Evans drumheads, Vic Firth sticks & mallets, Peripole-Bergerault educational instruments and Audio-Technica microphones. Others include Boomwhackers® Tuned Percussion Tubes, Lucinda Ellison Musical Instruments (Embira), Joia Tubes, and Shakka Shakerz. Find out more about Kalani at KalaniMusic.com.

My mission is simple— to help people play together.
—Kalani

Contents

Acknowledgements

This work represents the creativity and input of many people. As it is in the circle, we all help each other and shape our experience together. I extend my heartfelt thanks to the following people for their contributions, time and attention.

My Orff Schulwerk instructors Doug Goodkin, Konnie Saliba, Sofia Lopez-Ibor, James Harding, Will Salmon.

Music educators who helped "road test" much of this material: Brenda Williams—Rockvale Elementary School, Rockvale, Tennessee; Joanne Cinti—William Street School, Lancaster, New York; Karen Williamson—Prairie Mountain School, Eugene, Oregon; Martha Evans Osborne—Patterson Elementary, Hillsboro, Oregon; Debbie Fahmie—Cypress Elementary, Kissimmee, Florida; Veronika Schultz—Lincoln Elementary School, Riverton, Wyoming; Kay Lovingood—Martinez Elementary, Martinez, Georgia; Joan Eckroth-Riley—Northridge Elementary, Bismarck, North Dakota; Sue Michiels—traveling teacher, Los Angeles, California; Margaret Jerz—Evergreen Elementary, Wasau, Wisconsin

Music therapists Michael Marcionetti, Barry Bernstein

Facilitators/Drummers: Jim Greiner, Randy Crafton, Christine Stevens, Matt Savage, Layne Redmond, Christo Pellani, Dror Sinai, Cameron Tummel, Holly Blue Hawkins, Sule Greg Wilson, Chris Reid, Dee La Borte, Happy Shel, John Yost, Kerry "Shakerman" Greene, Kim Atkinson.

Babatunde Olatunji "Baba" 1927–2003. We miss you.

My training partner, Janet Marinaccio, for her ideas, work and guidance in producing this book and training programs.

Arthur Hull, who has contributed so much to the field of drum circle facilitation. Arthur is a valued teacher and friend and has helped me and many others with our musical mission. He has a unique facilitation method that he calls "Arthurian," and has shared his passion for drumming with hundreds of people throughout the world. His book is called *Drum Circle Spirit*.

No matter what accomplishments you make, somebody helped you.
—Althea Gibson

Julie Homi, Alisa Blackwood, Betty Ann Bruno, Russell Bruno, and Kellee McQuinn for their editorial assistance and ideas.

Dr. Rene Boyer for her friendship, help and guidance.

Gregg Charron and Gretchen Neilson at the Los Angeles Philharmonic's Partnership in Education Program.

Sylvia and Andrew Perry, Cak Marshall, Ralph Hicock & staff at Peripole-Bergerault, Inc. (Peripole.com)

Ken Fredenberg, Derek Zimmerman, Kim Graham, and Nikki Nearing at Toca Percussion. (TocaPercussion.com)

Victor Filanovich, David McAllister, Jim Rockwell, and Jennifer Ritz Latin Percussion. (LPMusic.com)

Michael Robinson and John Roderick at Evans Drum Heads. (EvansDrumheads.com)

Vic Firth, Tracy Firth, Neil Larravee, and Marco Soccoli at Vic Firth sticks & mallets. (VicFirth.com)

Craig Ramsell at Boomwhackers® Percussion Tubes. (WhackyMusic.com)

Rick Kramer at Joia Tubes. (Joia.com)

Dave Black, Kim Kasabian, Kate Westin, Andrew Surmani and everyone at Alfred Publishing. (Alfred.com)

Special thanks to the following people who contributed some really wonderful photos: Davis Bell, Bob De Mattina, Larry Kaptain, Ralph Hicock, Andrew Perry, Janet Marinaccio, Margaret Jerz, Craig Scheiner, Dave Black, Rob Heskett.

Introduction

Together in Rhythm is designed to help anyone create fulfilling music-based events for all kinds of people. It includes techniques, theories, knowledge, philosophies, activities, tools and resources that form a comprehensive approach to music facilitation. The information is presented in an easy-to-follow format that can be quickly applied to a wide variety of music-related professions including education, therapy and recreation.

The book will help you to

- improve your presentation and communication skills;

- gain confidence in working with various groups of people;

- learn about drums and percussion instruments;

- increase your musical skills, techniques and creative ideas;

- plan, organize, promote and present a rhythm-based event;

- create music in your school, community center, workplace or home.

The DVD will help you to

- see a drum circle in action;

- learn the facilitation techniques with more depth and understanding;

- gain new insights into the dynamics of group music making;

- develop creative ideas you can use in your own circles;

- experience the Drum Circle Music philosophy and approach.

If you are a **music educator** or **music therapist**, you will find that Drum Circle Music supports the goals and standards of your profession and provides useful activities that can easily be incorporated into your work. If you are **new to drum circles** or even to music at all, this book will provide you with everything you need to facilitate group music making with confidence. If you are an **experienced drum circle facilitator**, you will find many valuable resources throughout this book that will help you take your art to the next level and beyond.

Symbols Used in This Book

The following icons appear throughout to indicate various categories of information. You can use them to quickly find the information you are looking for.

About the DVD

The companion DVD is a wonderful educational resource that places you in the middle of the action and provides a wealth of information and ideas. There are four main subject areas: drum circle activities, drum circle games (games are more structured than activities), a world percussion guide with playing examples, and inspirational interviews with drum circle participants and Kalani.

The activities are enhanced with Drum Circle Music Iconography (DCMI), which appears in the upper-left corner of the screen to provide a visual guide that matches the cues of the facilitator.

Note: There are many activities on the DVD—far more than you would typically present in a program. They are separated by titles and occasional interviews (where extended periods of playing would take place).

Gain support for your programs by presenting portions of the DVD to your fellow teachers, co-workers, or funding organizations. Students will find it captivating and inspirational as well.

Tip: Copy the Instrument Guide folder to your computer and set it up as a slideshow or screensaver!

Drum Circle Music
Used for general and fundamental information.

Technology
Used for organizational and technical aspects.

Heart
Used for stories and personal aspects.

Creativity
Used for creative and inspirational aspects.

Quotes and Haikus

You will find inspirational quotes and haikus throughout the book that offer insight and reinforcement into the core message of the material.

 # Why Music?

It was the first day of a ten-week L.A. Philharmonic Artist in Residency program in which I was to teach music and movement to Los Angeles Public School third-graders who would otherwise have had little or no music education in their curriculum.

I began my first class by guiding about 40 students in an imaginary bubble exercise. We floated in our "bubbles," tossed them in the air, bounced them to the beat of a frame drum, and finally waved goodbye to them as we watched them float away into the sky. We used both our voices and our bodies to make music, reciting rhythmic syllables like *ta, ta, ti-ti, ta,* and filled the large room with hand clapping, finger snapping and foot stamping. I showed the children different ways to make sounds on my drum—striking it with a wooden beater, using my palm for a softer tone, and rubbing my finger on the skin to make the drum "sing." We all moved freely around the room in rhythm, sometimes alone, sometimes with a partner, but always to the beat of the drum. Students took turns leading the group while the others echoed the leader. At the end of the session, when I asked the children if there was anything they had particularly liked about the class, *everyone* said they liked playing with the "bubbles." Before it was time to leave, a girl put up her hand and bluntly asked, "Why are we learning music?"

"Well," I replied, after taking a moment to gather my thoughts, "believe it or not, music will help you with everything else you are learning in your life. It will help you with fractions in math, when you get to them. It will help you with geometry too, because music is written in dots that form lines and shapes. If you participate in sports or dancing, music will help you with your coordination and timing.

"Music will help you understand history, because composers often wrote about what mattered to them at the time. And because every culture on the planet has music, you can learn something about how people from other countries think and feel. You don't even need to know their language to speak to them through music.

"Music will help you learn how to get along with others because you have to listen carefully, and everyone likes a good listener. Music will help you become a creative, flexible thinker because when you improvise, or make up music on the spot, you will come up with new ways to do things. In fact, music is the only art form that is created *in the moment* and can be shared by an entire group of people at the same time. And most of all," I concluded, "Music is fun!"

"Okay," she said with a smile.

As I came to the end of my impromptu lecture, I realized I got a little carried away with my enthusiasm for music, and was filled with a sense of gratitude for the opportunities I've been given as an educator and facilitator to share my experience with others.

Chapter 1

 # What Is a Drum Circle?

A drum circle is a musical gathering. But a drum circle is more than just the instruments and the act of drumming; it is also the shared experience of the participants. The drums and drumming are the vehicles that take the group to its final destination—a place where everyone has a voice and is empowered to use it, and where the creative spirit is shared by everyone in the circle. A drum circle is really a *people circle*.

Drum circles are a form of *recreational music making*, which means that the focus is not on performance but rather on personal or group development and wellness, or just plain fun. The word *recreational* actually means "refreshment of strength and spirits after work." Playing music that renews our spirits is recreational.

> *I see their souls, and I hold them in my hands, and because I love them they weigh nothing.*
>
> **—Pearl Bailey**

Recreational music making is

- less about playing tunes and more about **tuning into our playfulness**;

- less about re-creating what others have done before and more about **co-creating** something **in the moment**;

- less about being on stage and more about reaching **new stages of being**;

- less about tuning out the environment and more about **tuning into your heart**.

Of course, the concept of recreational music making is nothing new. Before there were televisions, video games and the Internet, people would often gather in a living room or porch to sing songs, play their favorite tunes and drum out the rhythms of the day on a washboard or bucket. Thankfully, we seem to be remembering the importance of taking time to create music in a social atmosphere once again.

A drum circle can be simply defined as "a group of people working together to create in-the-moment music using drums and percussion instruments." Key words and phrases are *group, working together, create,* and *in-the-moment*. A drum circle is not a percussion ensemble performing a prepared piece of music, or a drumming class led by a teacher, nor any group that is re-creating music it has played before. It's a unique event that is spontaneously created by the participants, preferably with the help of a facilitator—a musical guide who helps the group achieve its goals.

When two people play drums together, each person is listening to the other, and they simultaneously create new music based on what they hear and feel. The music from one player enters the other through the ears, travels through the heart, and flows back out through the instrument to the first player. This process can be thought of as an *infinite rhythm loop* that connects people through a dynamic process of communication and expression.

When an entire group of people participate in the same process, a *rhythmic web* is created that serves to support and connect everyone in the group.

What Does a Facilitator Do?

A drum circle has the **potential** to accomplish many things, but it won't necessarily produce specific results without an experienced *facilitator*. A facilitator is not only a musician and teacher who guides the group through a process of *inclusion, cooperation* and *appreciation*, but is also caring and compassionate with the training and experience to help the group reach its goals.

The role of the facilitator is to

- provide an atmosphere that helps people feel welcome;

- help participants play music together;

- present activities that are fun and accessible;

- encourage creativity and cooperation;

- foster a sense of appreciation.

Nothing liberates our greatness like the desire to help, the desire to serve.

—Marianne Williamson

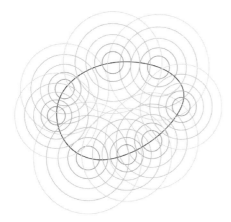

If the group falls out of sync...

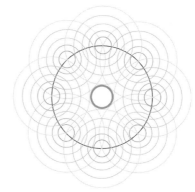

... the facilitator can step in and help them regain balance.

Are There Different Kinds of Drum Circles?

Yes, and they attract people for a variety of reasons, though of course there are universal qualities such as sharing, cooperation and focusing on a common goal. Some general categories include the following:

Community drum circles

Educational drum circles

Training & Development drum circles

Health & Wellness drum circles

Community Drum Circles

Drum circles take place in parks, beaches, community centers, music stores, sacred sites, and homes. All kinds of people participate in community drum circles, from those who have some drumming experience and want to play their drum for a couple of hours to those who are looking for a doorway into the world of music making and find drumming both intriguing and accessible. Still, there are those who gather for spiritual reasons and others who are simply looking for an opportunity to socialize or try something different and be exposed to new ideas and people.

Benefits of a community drum circle include

- new opportunities for socializing and making friends;
- an outlet for creativity and a forum for community music making;
- an open door to people who may not otherwise play music;
- a setting for spiritual growth and practice.

Educational Drum Circles

Music educators hold drum circles in classrooms, playgrounds and multi-purpose rooms. These circles are geared towards helping children discover the joys of creating their own music through exploration, play and active participation. Educational drum circles often focus on learning about the principles of music; the development of social skills such as sharing, listening and cooperation; and allowing students multiple avenues of expression. Educational drum circles may also include music games with specific themes or goals and may extend into other disciplines such as creative movement, singing and the visual arts.

Benefits of an educational drum circle include

- encouraging students to participate in ways that are right for them, which helps them gain confidence through positive experiences;
- allowing for a *multiple intelligence* (see page 56) approach by which students learn through exploration and the child's uniqueness is celebrated;
- placing the teacher in the role of a musical coach rather than a leader, allowing more freedom to observe and assess student progress.

Training & Development Drum Circles

Drum circles are used in business and professional settings as a developmental tool to illustrate the principles and advantages of teamwork, the value of diverse abilities, and the benefits of developing camaraderie among co-workers. Many corporations seeking to provide beneficial activities for their employees look to drum circles as a way to promote a sense of partnership, reduce stress, and encourage healthy peer relationships.

Benefits of training & development drum circles include

- illustrating the benefits of diversity;

- showing that by cooperating, people can achieve more together than they could alone (*synergy*);

- new and strengthened peer relationships, created through cooperation, that carry over into the workplace.

Health & Wellness Drum Circles

There are two main types of health-oriented drum circles: those used for therapy and those used for fitness. Therapists, counselors and healthcare workers use drum circles as music-based interventions when working with clients in a variety of settings, from in-patient mental health clinics to wellness centers. The focus can range from the development of fine or gross motor skills to helping clients with issues of self-esteem, cognitive functions, communication, impulse control, and coping or social skills.

Health and fitness applications are for people who enjoy active music making and the benefits gained from participating in a health-oriented drumming program. These include programs designed with physical and mental benefits in mind, and are best suited for recreational facilities, schools, and health clubs. Participants may experience benefits similar to those of practicing yoga, aerobics or meditation.

Benefits of health & wellness drum circle include

- a supportive environment for creative expression;

- opportunities for communication without using words;

- potential for improved physical, emotional and mental development.

Note: Facilitators who present outcome-oriented programs such as those used for music therapy, education, or corporate training typically have credentials and/or training in those fields. Effectively facilitating programs for specific populations not only requires an intimate understanding of their needs, concerns, and desired outcomes, but the ability to produce results through the implementation of a thoughtfully designed program. Facilitators who do not have specific training for the population they are serving are advised to work alongside a trained professional or seek training in that field.

 # Why Drums?

Percussion instruments were the first musical tools people created for use in group music making. They comprise the largest family of instruments, and virtually every culture on earth has some form of drumming. People all over the world use drums to celebrate life, explore their creativity, and unite in rhythm.

One of the best reasons to use drums is that they are accessible to most of us. Most people can find a drum or percussion instrument that suits their style. From beating out the pulse on a bass drum to adding a light shaker part, there's something for everyone in the world of percussion. From the earliest percussion gesture—striking two sticks or rocks together—to the use of specialized instruments such as congas and jembes, drums have provided people of all ages and abilities access to music making.

As one drum circle participant commented, "You never see a group of keyboardists jamming together, and even three guitar players in a room often can't get along, but you can have a group of 20, 30 or even 50 drummers playing together and they'll ask for more to join."

Drums are truly instruments of the people.

We use drums because they

- work well in large numbers;
- are generally inexpensive and easy to find or make;
- provide open access to music making;
- are portable, durable and convenient to store;
- offer variety and flexibility.

 ♡ From Teacher to Facilitator

I was presenting a series of world drumming classes at the Summer Percussion Institute in Taipei, Taiwan. For two weeks, I taught five classes a day: three for elementary school children, one for middle school kids, and one for high school students. After about a week of working with the younger children (ages 7 to 11), I noticed that they were feeling a little overwhelmed by the technical aspects of drumming, and I wanted to offer them something different to revitalize the learning atmosphere. I decided to ask the students to make up their own music using the skills they had learned during the first week. I believed the children were ready for such a challenge.

During the second week, my classes took on an entirely new shape. Rather than showing the students what to play by "teaching" them their parts, I divided the class into small groups and gave each group the following assignment: to create an original piece of music that has a beginning, a middle and an end, using any techniques they'd learned, rhythms they liked to play, and instrument combinations they preferred. I allowed them only ten minutes to create these pieces. As I moved from group to group, offering help where it was needed, the excitement in the room was palpable. Having felt somewhat worn out myself from an intensive week of lectures and demonstrations, I was now newly energized by the children's enthusiasm. At the end of the allotted preparation time, each group performed its original piece for the rest of the class.

I was amazed by the passion and creativity the students displayed—they came up with some really great stuff! All it took was setting the creative ball in motion, allowing them to create their own music. I decided to call this format the Jamnasium, because it reminded me of my experience in teaching gymnastics to children: we used our skills to "play" our way through the gym, but instead of working only on physical coordination, we were also developing rhythmic coordination and musical strengths.

Most importantly, by letting go of the teacher role, I became a musical *facilitator*, guiding the students to develop and express their own ideas. I discovered that the children had plenty to say and were capable of coming up with many different ways of saying it. All they needed was the opportunity and encouragement to express themselves by creating their own music.

When I returned to the States, I continued to develop the Jamnasium concept, adding games and combining music with movement activities. A couple of years later, Sylvia and Andrew Perry of Peripole-Bergerault (makers of educational instruments) introduced me to *Orff Schulwerk*, a holistic approach to music and movement education started by Carl Orff and Gunild Keetman, also known as *Music for Children*. The philosophies of the Orff approach aligned perfectly with those of the Jamnasium and Drum Circle Music, one of the primary objectives being to let the children be their own composers. Now a student of Orff Schulwerk, I encourage others to discover the many gifts it has to offer for it has helped me grow as a teacher, facilitator and a musician. To find out more about the Orff Schulwerk approach to music and movement education, visit AOSA.org.

What Is Drum Circle Music?

When I first started to facilitate group music making in the early 1990s, there wasn't a lot of information available on the subject. The drum circle was still emerging as a commonly accepted form of recreation and development, still shaking off the stigmatic dust of primal gatherings of sweaty men pounding out their anger around a blazing fire. I was still doing a lot of touring and recording, but there was something about the in-the-moment nature of music facilitation that intrigued me. I can recall times when I was recording movie soundtracks with large orchestras at Capitol Records and Paramount Pictures where I felt detached from my fellow musicians, "connected" only by the web of headphones that all lead back to the central click track. I

can remember concerts with both Yanni and Barry Manilow where we played to audiences of more than 15,000 people, and yet the feeling on stage was like being in a fish bowl—transparent, yet separated from the real world. To me, the *real world* of music is where the people are. When I work with people, I feel connected to them in a meaningful way. I love the communication, spontaneity and creativity that happens when a group of people who have never played together pick up a bunch of instruments and go for it.

My interest in music facilitation grew largely out of my role as a teacher and clinician. As the primary percussion clinician for TOCA Percussion, I have traveled around the U.S., visiting music stores and turning people on to hand percussion. As my format evolved from a clinic (lecture style) to more of a jam session (circle style), I noticed that when people had the opportunity to hold and play the instruments, even though they had no experience, their excitement and enthusiasm level shot up ten-fold. People were having a great time making up their own music (with a little help from me). The TOCA Percussion JamShop program (as we called it) was the first recreational drumming program in the U.S. and helped thousands of people get plugged in to drumming and active music making.

The more experienced I became at music facilitation, the more questions I had. (Isn't it always like that?) Why did some events *feel* better than others? Are there

universal principles that work for every population? What are the best ways to deal with problems that come up? What are the structural elements that need to be present? What is the best way to provide participants with guidance without restricting them? How do I help the experience carry over into people's lives?

Though I had many of my own "facilitator's" questions, there were many other "beginner's" questions coming from teachers, therapists, musicians, and people interested in music facilitation: Can I facilitate even though I'm not a drummer? What instruments should I use? How should I set up my drum circle? Are there specific beats that people play? How long should a drum circle be? What should I do for a children's drum circle? Can anyone do this?

It seemed that many people were interested in creating music making opportunities for others, but didn't know where to start. I added their questions to mine and over the next few years started to develop the Drum Circle Music approach. Many of the answers to my questions came through creating activities and games for the hundreds of sessions I presented in the schools, working with multi-generational populations during TOCA Percussion JamShops in music stores all over the United States and creating training materials for the many sessions I presented at state and national conferences for music educators. I also gained insights into the art of facilitation through creating outcome-oriented programs such as Tashiko Fitness Drumming, which I presented at my local gym. But Drum Circle Music was not developed without the contributions and insights of the many talented musicians, teachers and facilitators who form the community of which I am fortunate to be a part. The process I experienced in developing this approach was a perfect analogy for the synergy that happens in a drum circle—many voices coming together to create something that is greater than the sum of its parts.

Drum Circle Music is a collection of knowledge, tools, activities, techniques and resources that can help anyone become an effective drum circle facilitator. It's a holistic approach to empowering groups of all kinds with ways to reach their full creative potential through *inclusion, cooperation* and *appreciation*. Drum Circle Music meets and supports the professional standards of music-related fields including music education and music therapy,

incorporating unique tools that provide for multiple learning styles and diverse populations. The books, video components, website and live training courses offer multiple levels of support that make learning and applying the Drum Circle Music approach both accessible and effective.

Drum Circle Music is comprehensive, addressing many aspects of music facilitation, from the physical nuts and bolts of choosing the right instruments and setting up an event to the finer aspects such as presenting compelling activities and games and helping people enjoy playing together.

Because it's not a method or strict protocol, Drum Circle Music can be easily adapted to suit all kinds of populations from children to the elderly, and from living rooms to board rooms. Whether you're a professional who wishes to incorporate drumming into your existing programs or intend to create a business centered around music facilitation, the principles, techniques, activities and philosophies of Drum Circle Music make it easy to reach your goals.

This book and DVD combination is a valuable resource that describes and shows many of the aspects of Drum Circle Music facilitation. It serves as both an introduction and reference guide to the approach; but just as the sounds of music do not come from the printed page, the heart and soul of Drum Circle Music does not exist in a book or a DVD. In a word, Drum Circle Music is about *people*. It is something that is to be experienced first hand.

Drum Circle Music training courses meet the highest standards of many music-related professions. They provide opportunities to experience Drum Circle Music in a supportive setting while learning from professionals. To find out more about the benefits of becoming a certified Drum Circle Music facilitator, see "Training Programs" on page 98 or visit DrumCircleMusic.com.

Who Can Become a Drum Circle Music Facilitator?

Drum Circle Music facilitation is about much more than inspiring others to take up drumming or even make music together. It's about inspiring a healthy lifestyle that includes self-expression, creativity and community. One of the first steps we can take towards creating a musically accessible society is to place the emphasis back on *play* rather than performance and focus on the *personal benefits* rather than the musical product.

Angeles Arrien, Ph.D., discusses the importance of a holistic approach to life and learning in her book *The Four Fold Way: Walking the Paths of the Warrior, Teacher, Healer, and Visionary* (San Francisco: HarperSanFrancisco, 1993).

> Every culture has many ways of maintaining health and well-being. Healers throughout the world recognize the importance of maintaining or retrieving the four universal healing salves: storytelling, singing, dancing and silence. Shamanic societies believe that when we stop singing, stop dancing, are no longer enchanted by stories, or become uncomfortable with silence, we experience soul loss, which opens the door to discomfort and disease. The gifted healer restores the soul through the use of the healing salves.

If you believe that making music is an essential element for maintaining health and well-being, then you can become a facilitator of HEALTHY LIVING.

Children often incorporate many forms of creativity into their daily life, humming melodies while dancing or playing games and creating their own rhymes and songs using their growing vocabulary. We naturally combine multiple aspects of artistic expression into our playtime activities when we are young. As we move through the formal education process, we may end up focusing on only one or two of these aspects such as instrumental music or dance. Many people give up playing music because they come to see it as an art discipline, reserved only for those with "talent." Because they fall out of the habit of *playing through* music, they lose their confidence with regards to their artistic abilities or—even worse—believe they can't play at all.

If you are excited at the thought of helping others to regain their child-like enthusiasm for creating music, then you can become a facilitator of EXPRESSION.

> *You can't put music into people, but you CAN help to bring it out.*
>
> **—Kalani**

Making music involves much more than simply playing an instrument. It's exploration, creativity, expression, communication, movement, speech, problem solving, listening, and celebrating. After I facilitated a drum circle at a music store in San Antonio, Texas, a young boy said to me, "When I started to play the drum, I felt like the real me." His statement illustrated that the drum circle helped him connect not only with the other participants, but also with himself. Studies show that people who participate in group music making are likely to have lower stress levels than people who don't. Perhaps it's because they are using music like children do—as a way to play with others, discover something about themselves, and enjoy life.

If you believe that making music can help people reduce stress and uncover their "real selves," then you can become a facilitator of SELF-DISCOVERY.

The research proves it—students who participate in music programs score higher on math, language and science tests than those who don't. Music students average higher SAT scores, regardless of their socioeconomic background. Studies show that adults benefit greatly from the social aspects of group music making.

If you believe that music plays an important role in our development and continued happiness in life, then you can become a facilitator of POTENTIAL.

Playing *through* music is one of the best ways people can connect with one another and share a common bond. It's a healthy way we can reach out to our neighbors, make new friends, and create a sense of community in a world in which people spend a lot of time looking into television and computer screens. Participating in group music-making activities is a great way to learn about ourselves and each other, gain confidence in our creative abilities, learn how to work together, reduce anxiety levels, and express ourselves in a way that is fundamental to who we are.

If you believe in the power of group music making to change people's lives for the better, then you can become a facilitator of Drum Circle Music.

If we are to inspire others to play, then we have to be the first to offer to play with them. It's up to us to lead by example, not only in our social and professional lives, but in our private lives as well. We have to walk our talk and dance our rhythms.

People naturally want to play, make up games and songs and share them with others. Just watch children playing together to confirm this. Was there a time in your life when you made up games, sang songs and were enchanted by the unknown? Are you still this way today? If not, why? By opening ourselves up to the child-like spirit that lies inside, we become connected to greater resources of joy, creativity and love that we share with all beings. Opening up to our creative spirit requires that we give ourselves and others permission to play, to be true to our nature, to be authentic.

A Contract with Myself

I promise to spend as much time as I can developing my capacity to play like a child by

✔ *drawing pictures of myself, my friends, my pets and my family;*

✔ *writing stories, poems and songs that only make sense to me;*

✔ *playing with clay, dough, sand, water or whatever I can find in the backyard;*

✔ *making music with my voice, body, stuff in my room, dog toys and anything else that makes a sound;*

✔ *dancing as if no one was watching;*

✔ *laughing out loud, especially at myself;*

✔ *following my intuition towards all things magical.*

*Signed*_____ *Date*_____

Always let them think of you as singing and dancing.

—Anita Brookner

Chapter 2

Philosophy and Approach

The structure of a Drum Circle Music event is built upon three key components that are essential to maximizing a successful group process: *inclusion, cooperation* and *appreciation*. Forming the structure of a Drum Circle Music experience, these three components are not separate events, but rather are interrelated and flow from one to another They are subtle but necessary for producing a sense of completeness. Structure is an indispensable ingredient in Drum Circle Music because it provides participants with a sense of belonging, community and reverence, which together form a complete experience for mind, body and spirit.

 Inclusion

KEY CONCEPTS
Accessibility • Equity • Security

Before we can work as a community, we have to become one. A group of people showing up in the same space at the same time is simply a crowd. A group of people working together with a common intention and understanding of purpose is a community. As a Drum Circle Music facilitator, your first objective with any group is to provide opportunities for each member to feel included from the onset. This process can take many forms, but the result is consistent: the participants are looking at and listening to one another, they are invested in the process, and they feel important.

inclusion cooperation

appreciation

The following table shows ways you can help create a sense of inclusion:

Intention	Action/Activity	Result
To focus the group's attention.	Move together in rhythm.	Everyone looks and listens.
To encourage participation.	Help people choose and play an instrument that's right for them.	Everyone feels like they can contribute.
To foster a sense of inclusiveness.	Acknowledge the participants.	Everyone feels involved.
To set the circle of spirit.	Welcome them into their circle.	Everyone feels like they belong there.
To connect the participants to each other.	Have them welcome, greet and acknowledge each other.	Everyone is united.
To provide a sense of security.	Let them know that there is no wrong way to play.	Everyone feels at ease.
To create an atmosphere of equity.	Announce intentions of sharing everyone's unique gifts.	Everyone feels valued.
To create a playful atmosphere..	Stop talking and start playing!	Everyone feels that they have permission to play.

Focus on the T.O.P.

Tools, not tasks

Options, not opinions

Process, not performance

Tools

The ultimate goal of a facilitator is to provide the group with a musical sand box, shovel, and water and then give them the space, time, and inspiration to help them build their own version of a musical castle. If you were to dictate exactly how they were to build that castle, you would reduce the ways in which they could contribute, thereby marginalizing their input and possibly leaving them feeling unimportant. By offering tools for self-expression, we empower participants with the means to explore their creativity in ways that are right for them. If and when they need more tools, we can provide them, but for the most part we want to stay out of their way and let them play. When participants build the music on their own, it belongs to them, and they will always make their best effort to take care of it. When joint ownership is felt by everyone involved, a community is created.

> *We want to create an atmosphere in which creation is possible.*
>
> **—Marie Rambert**

Drumming, though accessible, is not always simple or easy. As a facilitator, you will be asked questions about different instruments and may be called upon to demonstrate certain playing techniques for your participants. Many percussion instruments require years of training and practice to play properly, but there are ways to work around traditional techniques, offering alternatives that allow anyone to start playing right away. Being able to help participants use the instruments is key to breaking down the physical barriers to a fulfilling experience and ensuring a safe and successful musical journey. See the section in Chapter 3 called "Everyone Can Make Music" for suggestions and ideas that will help you help others to make music together.

Circle Empowerment

I had just finished presenting a Jamnasium (an improvised exploration of music through games and activities) at the Seattle World Rhythm Festival. The group consisted of 75 third-graders from several local schools. A colleague of mine approached me after the session and said, "I guess you can see that some things don't work too well with every group." He was referring to a point in one of the games where communication broke down between the participants and we had to start the activity over. We were playing a game called "Orbit," based on the "Telephone" game where a sound or phrase is passed around the circle from one person to the next. I suppose from a performance point of view one could say that it didn't work too well because the chain of rhythm was broken and we had to start over. What my colleague didn't see (or notice) was that when the orbit was broken, I stopped and asked the students a few questions:

Facilitator: What happened?

Students: The rhythm fell apart.

Facilitator: Why?

Students: Because some people were not paying attention.

Facilitator: So, what do we need to do to make it better?

Students: Be ready and listen to the person next to you.

The kids had fixed their own problem. Now they understood why it's so important for everyone to pay attention and work together and they didn't hear it from me as an adult or teacher. They were not made to feel like they messed up or failed. They were empowered to improve and they did. The next time through the game went perfectly. The children felt good about the outcome, perhaps even more accomplished than they might have if the game had gone perfectly the first time.

The real problem was not that the chain was broken the first time through, but that one of my peers had placed more value on the performance than on the process of learning and working together. As far as I was concerned, our orbit game was a great success and worked very well. After all, what is a game for if not to teach us how to work together?

Options

There are many ways to play and none of them are wrong. For example, you can play a conga drum with your hands, sticks or mallets, rap on the shell with your knuckles, or scratch the head with your fingertips. As facilitators, our goal is to help people with their process of discovery by encouraging participants to share their ideas and allowing them the freedom to discover, on their own, what works for them and what doesn't. By presenting options, we allow participants to follow the path that feels right for them, providing the means to go to that place where they feel authentic and free. Some of these include the following:

Technique—by pointing out common techniques for playing the instruments and offering various sticks, mallets and beaters that can help people play drums without using their hands.

Music making—by using accessible terms to refer to the elements of music and providing ways for people to learn the basic language of music without the need for formal study.

Personal development—by providing a safe and supportive environment that encourages self-expression, exploration and the sharing of ideas.

Process

The primary role of the facilitator is to help the group reach its full potential by guiding it through a thoughtfully designed process, presented with care and compassion. A facilitator helps the group reach its highest potential by observing, asking questions, presenting options and staying in the present moment. By focusing on the process of group cooperation rather than the product of the musical performance, we encourage participants to create an experience that is truly their own, providing just the right amount of input, support and release to help them reach their full potential.

> *Listen long enough and the person (group) will generally come up with an adequate solution.*
>
> **—Mary Kay Ash**

A group has the potential to

- uncover the music they feel inside by offering accessible tools for self-expression;

- develop a sense of cooperation, creativity and group spirit that transcends the boundaries of language, age, culture, race and economic status;

- create the physical and emotional space for connecting with themselves and each other through appreciation and sharing.

How do we know if we are succeeding?

We know we are succeeding when we see smiles and hear a joyful noise.

> *Listening is not merely not talking, though even that is beyond most of our powers; it means taking a vigorous, human interest in what is being told us.*
>
> **—Alice Deur Miller**

 # Cooperation

KEY CONCEPTS
Balance • Communication • Teamwork

Cooperation may be defined as "working together to reach a common goal." When everyone feels invested in the process and owns it, they exert their greatest efforts to create the best possible outcome with the other participants. Success is not determined by outcome alone, however, but by the willingness and ability of the participants to work together. There may be times when there is a lack of understanding, communication or focus; there might even be a breakdown of a particular activity, but the process is still one of cooperation if the willingness to work together remains.

Intention	Action/Activity	Result
To create an atmosphere that feels welcoming.	Allow participants to contribute in a way that works for them.	Everyone feels a sense of creative freedom.
To encourage full participation from everyone in the group.	Supply as many options as possible for interaction.	Everyone finds a way to integrate into the experience.
To offer tools for personal and group development.	Create systems where communication is key.	The group has new ways to learn and grow together.
To create opportunities for teamwork and collaboration.	Present music games and goal-oriented activities.	Everyone works together towards a common goal.
To draw ideas from the participants.	Observe, listen and reflect ideas back to the group.	The group creates their own music.
To offer alternatives for participation.	Present vocal chants, body percussion, and alternative ways to play the instruments.	Everyone can be themselves and bonds become strong.
To help participants realize their highest potential.	Amplify what works and encourage listening.	Participants reach new levels of expression and communication.

How May I Help?

By asking yourself the question, "How may I best serve this group at this time?" you stay focused on the goals of the group rather than on your own agenda. I'm not suggesting you literally ask everyone how you may help them. Discovering the best way to serve the group can take the form of offering an activity and observing how the group responds. If it works for the group, then your intuition was good. If the group seems to have trouble with it, then you have the option of trying something else. What you don't want to do is take the attitude of "We're going to get this right if it's the last thing we do!" Why? Because it really doesn't matter what the specific activity or outcome is. All that matters is that it's something that resonates with the participants and allows them the security and freedom to express whatever it is they want to express. If everyone is engaged and having fun, then you have answered the question. You have helped them become a healthy, creative community by serving them in the best way possible.

> *To show a child what once delighted you, to find the child's delight added to your own–this is happiness.*
>
> **—J. B. Priestley**

Point of Origin

As a facilitator, you may take time to examine your own process during an event. The ultimate goal is to create an atmosphere where you are allowing most of the ideas to come from the group. Effective facilitation requires asking oneself the question, "Am I leading the group or helping them lead themselves?" One of the keys to understanding this is to examine the *point of origin* of an activity. Did the ideas for the activity come from you, the facilitator, or did they come from the participants? By opening up the floor to new ideas, you increase the creative potential of the experience by the number of people in the group. Thirty people in the circle means that there are 30 creative minds, 30 creative spirits and 30 possible directions in which the group could move at any given moment. It can be tempting to constantly hand out parts for the group to play or suggest specific activities—and in some instances, that may be appropriate; but every circle of people is a vast resource for creative ideas that are just waiting to be discovered and set free with your help. You truly facilitate the group's musical process when you use and develop ideas that originate in the minds and spirits of the participants.

HAIKU

Time to make a change
Listen to their ideas
For inspiration

Drawing Ideas from the Group

You can draw ideas from the group by following this simple three-step approach:

1. Create space for new ideas to emerge by not teaching or leading the group.

2. Observe the participants by looking, listening and using your intuition.

3. Reflect and amplify creative elements back to the group.

Reflecting an idea can be a simple act such as pointing to an instrument someone is playing as if to say, "Hey everyone, listen to this!" (Never point at someone directly, as this may cause some people to feel uncomfortable, but rather to the instrument.) Another way is to amplify an idea through matching what someone else is playing. This reinforces the idea and draws attention to it, allowing others the opportunity to join in and play along.

To me education is a leading out of what is already there in the pupil's soul.
—Muriel Spark

The Balancing Point

As part of Drum Circle Music training, I often have participants take part in what I call the *Trio Dance*: three people moving together while the leadership role is constantly changing among them. From the perspective of the person who is watching the dance, it looks like the group is performing a choreographed sequence of movements, but it is simply the changing dynamics between the three people that allows the group to function as one body. There are times in a drum circle where inspiration strikes, creating magical moments and a special feeling of connection between the participants. No one was leading, yet everyone was in rhythm with each other and seemed to know what the others were going to do before they did it. The key to successful drum circle facilitation is maintaining the *balancing point* between the leadership role of the facilitator, the collective direction of the participants, and the inspirational moments, as they follow each other and move as one.

Plan Not to Have a Plan

Somewhere between leading and following is facilitation. Facilitating is like dancing—taking turns leading, following, and responding to the other in the moment. It is important that you always use your abilities to facilitate the group's music and not simply move through a pre-planned routine. The group will let you know when they are ready for a change or a more challenging setting. If you are planning, you can't be in the moment. As with the Trio Dance, all you have to do is observe and be ready to move with the group.

> *We ought to be careful not to do for the group only what we intended to help them do.*
> **—Frank A. Clark**

Holly Blue Hawkins discusses a key concept for the art of facilitation in her book *The Heart of the Circle: A Guide to Drumming* (Freedom: Crossing Press, 1999).

> Leadership is a skill that needs to be learned. So is followership. Many of us equate leading with control and following with submission or powerlessness, but this is not necessarily so. Both roles can empower one another in a relationship based on partnership.

 **Appreciation**

KEY CONCEPTS
Reflection • Integration • Gratitude

In order to gain the full benefit from the time we spend together, a portion of that time may be set aside to acknowledge everyone's unique contribution through brief statements, moments of reflections and actions of gratitude. Ending an event through appreciation allows participants to reflect on their experience and gain personal insights and lessons from the time they shared with the group. It also helps people come down from a "drummer's high" and land softly back on earth. Most importantly, it's a time for everyone to strengthen bonds and make lasting connections with the other members of the circle.

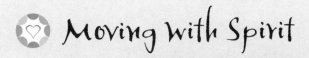 Moving with Spirit

The tip of the canoe split the glass-like surface of the lake, sending out ripples like giant wings that extended into the morning mist. My paddle rhythmically dipped into the water, sending me gliding forward through the cool air. I imagined I was paddling with my ancestors across the ocean. What an amazing feeling to sit in a dug-out canoe with five other people, paddles moving in perfect synchronization as we darted through the water. I could feel my paddle break the surface, splashing a bit each time, then there was no sound. When my paddle was in perfect sync with the speed of the canoe there was no splash, just a brief moment of acceleration as the power from my body was transferred to the canoe. I had noticed this feeling before when I drummed. When our rhythms lined up perfectly there was no sound from an individual, just the group sound, the power from my drum joining with all the others to move the rhythm forward—without a splash. Those are the magic moments, when we become one with the group—and the group becomes one with us. When we are in harmony with our environment we feel the power of synergy, of working together and becoming something much bigger than ourselves.

When closing the circle, you may encourage statements of appreciation by asking questions such as these:

- Did you see anyone doing anything you particularly liked?
- What are some moments you will remember from this experience?
- Do you feel differently now than when you first started to play?
- How will you incorporate the lessons you learned in the circle into your daily life?
- What is the story you would tell someone else about this experience?

Note: Be sure to appreciate yourself, your unique gifts, and your commitment to helping others!

Intention	Action/Activities	Result
To set the circle for closing.	Look, listen and move together, hold hands, breathe.	Everyone is focused in the moment.
Help the circle learn from itself.	Acknowledge and introduce elders in the community.	Everyone gains insights from the wisdom of the group.
To create a sense of appreciation.	Thank everyone for playing and learning together.	Everyone feels appreciated.
To acknowledge the importance of diversity.	Acknowledge the variety of participants, pointing out that each contributed something different and important.	Everyone feels they have a unique gift to offer and that they have been accepted for who they are.
To learn from the group experience.	Reflect upon experiences, drawing analogies to other aspects of life.	Activities are processed through appreciation and lead to knowledge and wisdom.
To reinforce the feeling of community between participants.	Introduce and thank all the people who organized and presented the event.	Participants feel a deeper connection to one another as contributions are acknowledged.
To encourage continued support between participants.	Allow time for announcements about upcoming events.	Everyone leaves with something to look forward to.
To deepen the experience.	Provide time for a silent or guided meditation or prayer.	Everyone has time to process personal thoughts and feelings.
To end the event.	Have participants thank one another before leaving.	Everyone feels energized and connected.

It is an illusion to think that more comfort means more happiness. Happiness comes of the capacity to feel deeply, to enjoy simply, to think freely, to be needed.

—Storm Jameson

Chapter 3

Making Music

The Instruments

Below is a brief guide to the instruments that are commonly used in drum circles. Additional instruments, descriptions, and pronunciations can be found in the Instrument Guide on page 85.

Categories of Instruments

Unpitched Percussion
  drums
  wood sounds
  shakers & scrapers
  metal sounds

Pitched Percussion

Body Percussion

Vocal Sounds

UNPITCHED PERCUSSION

 Drums

Bass Drums (low pitch, played with sticks or mallets)

dundun

harmony drums

surdo

Hand Drums (played with the hands)

ashiko

bongos

conga

doumbek

jembe

Cajón

Frame Drums (played with hands, sticks or mallets)

various frame drums

 Wood Sounds

clapper sticks

clave

two-tone blocks

slit drum

temple blocks (tone blocks)

woodblock

Shakers & Scrapers

axatse

cabasa

caxixi

egg shakers

frogs & crickets

guiro

reco-reco

maracas

shékere

tube shakers

 ## Metal Sounds

agogo, cowbell, gankogui

finger cymbals, pagoda bells (Tibetan bells), triangle,

jingle stick, sleigh bells, tambourine

gong

wind chimes

 ## PITCHED PERCUSSION

barred (Orff instruments)

Boomwhackers® Percussion Tubes

Joia Tubes

kalimba

BODY PERCUSSION

clap

pat (or *patschen*, meaning "patting the leg")

snap

stamp

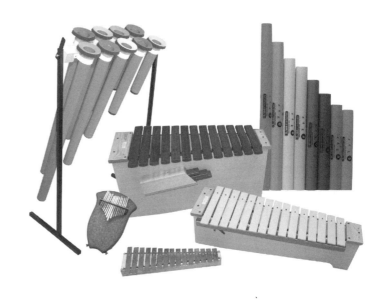

VOCAL SOUNDS

chanting

singing

toning

Everyone Can Make Music

One of the best ways you can help people make their own music is to provide them with tools that are easy to use. Many people associate learning how to *play* music with learning how to *read* music. This is unfortunate, as not knowing how to read music is often used as an excuse to not play music. For this reason, we want to emphasize playing first and focus on learning to read notation second.

The following are simple musical concepts you can use in your circles right away that don't require any formal musical training for your participants. They include four *modes of play*—rolling, riding, riffing, and resting—examples of what players can do with their own instrument, and three *modes of interaction*—match, echo, and answer—which are ways someone can relate to what someone else is playing.

 ## Modes of Play

KEY CONCEPTS
Familiarity • Accessibility • Simplicity

Rolling

Rolling is something we can all do naturally. It's a steady stream of notes, in or out of rhythm, usually made with an alternating motion. It is as natural as walking. I often have the group experience free-rolling (rumbling) as a way to explore the instruments and dynamics. Learning to roll is like learning to walk.

Example: I might ask, "See how many different sounds you can make on your instrument," then invite people to look around and observe how others are playing their instruments. It's really amazing to see how creative some people can be when they don't know the "correct" way to play something! It's also a great lesson for those of us who may think we know how an instrument *should* be played. Freedom is what rolling is all about.

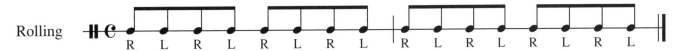

Riding

Riding is playing a specific pattern that repeats. Just as we may learn how to skip, hop, walk sideways or move in any other way that differs from normal walking, we may also explore different ways of moving in rhythm. Perhaps the simplest way of creating a riding pattern (often called an *ostinato* in formal music settings) is to start off with a rhythmic roll, then remove a couple of the notes so a specific pattern emerges. As a facilitator, you can help provide a vocabulary of riding patterns for your participants by having them echo your patterns or those played by someone else in the group.

Once, when I was presenting a drum circle at a music store in Colorado, we created drum patterns from the names of two of the young participants. The title of our new rhythm was a combination of both their names. Not only did we create cool-sounding music, but I think they felt a special kind of pride knowing that we used their names for inspiration.

Tip: For special occasions such as birthdays, or to honor members of your group, make up rhythms from their names, what they like, or things they have accomplished. This way the music is original, specific to the members of the group and the occasion.

Riffing

Riffing is often called *soloing* or *improvising*, meaning it doesn't follow a set pattern but still relates to the music and underlying rhythms. Riffing doesn't have to be fancy, fast or complicated, just done with good intentions. You may wish to provide some time for the members of your group to riff by featuring them individually at a certain time during the event; however, it's always a good idea to let people choose whether they want to riff or not. Many are very happy to simply roll along in rhythm.

Riffing

Resting

We are resting when we are actively listening and creating space in the music for something else to be heard. Resting does not mean "not participating." It means intentionally clearing room in the music or *playing the space*. Resting is also a way to change the dynamics of the group and to give people's hands a break from playing. I often make a "now-let's-listen-to-them-play" gesture after I've stopped part of the group to let the people who are resting know they have something to do that is just as important as the people who are still playing: **listening**!

Participants may be reminded that they can do two out of four of these, rolling and resting, right from the start. I like to ask participants to provide their own examples of rolling, riding and riffing for each other rather than demonstrate them myself. This helps participants contribute to the learning process and demonstrates the fact that making music is not mysterious or complicated, but is something we all intrinsically know how to do.

> **Tip:** People who are resting can show their appreciation for those who are playing by clapping along in rhythm or greeting their playing with cheers and encouragement.

Modes of Interaction

KEY CONCEPTS
Non-verbal • Sharing • Flexible

Once we know how to move on our own, the next step is learning how to move with others. Moving with a partner or an entire group of partners is at the core of what group drumming is about. Participating in a shared, rhythmic dance involves using our social and intuitive skills to look, listen, and flow with others. The following tools provide participants with ways to make connections with the other participants, increase their rhythmic vocabulary and learn how to play together. By introducing these simple tools to your group, you empower them (and yourself) to start making music right away.

Matching [ ]

Matching is to align, pair or harmonize within an exact manner. When we copy someone else and do what he or she is doing, we are matching. *Entrainment* (moving together) is a form of matching. Most players will match many aspects of the music—such as volume and tempo—automatically, so pointing out the many possible ways a particular rhythm or tonal pattern can be matched will help participants reach deeper into the music and connect with one another on more levels than they may have imagined. I often point out that any two instruments can match each other, even if they are not from the same timbre group or are played in very different ways as are a cowbell and a conga drum. Rhythms can be matched as well as volume and pitch. Playing can also be matched in movements and body language (more on that in Facilitation Cues).

> **Tip:** During a break in the music, suggest that each player match someone else in the group the next time they start to play. Later on, ask them if the music felt different during that period. How did it feel? What caused the change?

Echoing

Echoing is defined as a repetition or imitation of another. An echo is essentially a matched pattern or phrase that is offset in time. By listening and echoing, participants may broaden their rhythmic vocabulary as they learn to listen to musical cues from the facilitator and/or other participants. By having the group echo a variety of short phrases, the facilitator can provide new musical ideas for the participants to use as riding or riffing patterns later on. Echoing combines resting, listening and playing.

Answering

Answering is giving a corresponding response to an action. Many styles of music incorporate the use of question and answer phrases between members of the group. One could think of an answer as an *echo riff*, a phrase that relates to another phrase but is not exactly the same. Answering, like echoing, presumes that resting (listening) occurs between players as one listens for the "question" before responding.

The Groove

KEY CONCEPTS
Simple • Solid • Supportive

> *It's always the simple that produces the marvelous.*
> **—Amelia Barr**

Most drum circle activities revolve around playing together in rhythm. Because rhythm is the part of music that pertains to forward motion, we must always do our best to maximize the participants' potential for success by providing tools and techniques that will make it easy for them to move forward together.

Creating a Solid Groove

- **Have a few key percussion parts.**

Have someone keep a steady beat on a cowbell or woodblock. Remind shaker and rattle players to use alternating motions (rolling) to keep patterns flowing and easy to play. Encourage simplicity and repetition.

- **Have bass drums support the pulse.**

When using more than one bass drum, ask players to play complementary parts (ones that balance each other by alternating or overlapping). Suggest that they accent the strong beats, e.g., the first and third of every four.

- **Keep additional percussion parts simple.**

Adding the smaller percussion instruments creates a "rhythmic grid" that will complement the pulse and help glue all the other parts together. Encourage patterns that are simple. *It's a gift to be simple!*

- **Add the hand drums last.**

Because hand drums are the only instrument group that is primarily played with both hands, parts can end up being very busy. Beginning with all the other instruments provides a solid foundation for the hand drummers that may encourage them to play simple parts with more built-in space.

Tip: To demonstrate the power and beauty of simplicity, play the music game Pieces of Eight on page 64.

Groove Review

When everyone's hands and hearts come together in time, the group feels the power of unity and the magic of synergy. As a facilitator, your role is often to find ways that help participants identify the pulse, hear it clearly, and play along with it. You can do this by helping them to play simple parts, focusing their attention to a supportive instrument (bass drum, shaker, bell), and playing a steady pulse on an instrument that is easy to hear. Though the ultimate goal of a Drum Circle Music session extends far beyond the musical product of the participants, helping everyone play together in time is part of the process. Falling into a groove allows everyone to feel that special sense of accomplishment and community when hands and hearts align.

Chapter 4

 # Facilitation Techniques

Effectively facilitating group music making requires the study, development and application of various techniques and *cues* used to guide groups through various *settings* and *segues*. For example, you may choose to have some people rest and listen while others play their instruments, suggest that everyone play softer, rotate the leadership role around the circle, or feature a single player. There are many possibilities within the drum circle format to create extemporaneous music that brings out the best in the participants and creates both inspiring and magical moments.

There are two ways to deliver the various types of cues to your group: verbally and non-verbally. Verbal instructions are best delivered when the group is not playing and the information is detailed, as in a music game. Non-verbal cues work best while the group is playing, with groups in which members do not all speak the same language, or for hearing-impaired or deaf participants. Non-verbal cues also allow you to save your voice because you don't have to shout to be heard over the instruments. They promote visual connections within the group and help keep participants tuned into the activities by encouraging them to focus on the facilitator and each other.

Key Facilitation Terms

Cue: A verbal or non-verbal signal or instruction given by the facilitator.

Setting: An arrangement of facilitated or non-facilitated musical activities. A setting can be thought of as a musical island, a place to explore before moving on.

Examples
- Everyone is playing softly.
- Only the people with shakers are playing while the others are listening.
- Half the circle is echoing the facilitator, while the other half is keeping the beat.

Segue: A facilitated transition used to connect settings. Think of a segue as a musical bridge, used to move from one setting to another.

Examples
- Speeding up the tempo.
- Moving from voices to instruments.
- Playing softer through echoing.

Body Language

Effectively cuing the group requires that you always have three elements present in your body language: *commitment*, *clarity* and *consistency*. By giving your cues with commitment, clarity and consistency, you maximize your effectiveness as a facilitator and help them move together in rhythm. Moving from one setting to another will feel like dancing with an experienced partner—natural, secure and flowing.

Commitment

You gain the support and trust of the participants by being present for the group and following through with your actions. If you're not focused on your work, or if your energy is low, the group may not feel a strong connection to you and may not respond well as a result. To be a successful facilitator, you have to give 110 percent to the circle all the time and be committed in everything you do.

Clarity

Having commitment without clarity is like delivering a compelling speech with a mouth full of crackers. You can have the best intentions, but if the participants can't understand what you are trying to convey to them, they will not be able to respond as a group. Effective cues convey meaning without words. Dancers and mimes do this as part of their art; as a facilitator, you will, too. Your body is your voice when you are facilitating; when you cue the group, do it with your legs, torso, arms, hands and eyes. Take your time and move with clarity, and the group will be with you all the way.

Consistency

It's not important that you cue a group the same way that another facilitator might cue them. What is important is that you are consistent within your own style. As you work with a group, its members will learn your style and become accustomed to your body language. Inconsistency can confuse some people, or it will at least consume valuable time as they learn your unfamiliar moves. Of course, there's nothing wrong with experimenting or trying something creative—just be sensitive to the needs of the participants and make sure your first priority is to help them play together.

 # DCMI (Drum Circle Music Iconography)

A special set of characters called *Drum Circle Music Iconography*, or *DCMI*, is used to visually represent most facilitation cues, musical elements and drum circle activities. DCMI icons are easy to read and write; they can help visual learners comprehend and remember sequences of cues, providing a way to visualize, notate and "chunk" combinations of cues without writing out long descriptions.

Here are some examples of DCMI that have been used in this book so far:

Rattles　　**Echo**　　**Drums**　　**Match**　　**Wood Sounds**

In this chapter, you will discover how to use DCMI to represent facilitation cues, segues and settings.

You can use DCMI to

- learn and remember drum circle activities;
- note your ideas or journal your experiences after an event;
- represent drum circle activities to other facilitators across the boundaries of language;
- integrate music and graphic arts.

A complete list of DCMI is provided in the appendix on page 97.

 # Setting a Cue

Before cuing the group, it's helpful to *set* your cue by getting the attention of the participants to let them know to get ready because something is coming up:

1. Move to the center of the circle so everyone can see you.
2. Hold up your hand(s) to let them know something is coming.
3. Make eye contact with as many people as possible.

Note: The larger the group, the more time you'll need to set your cues, allowing adequate time to gain people's attention. For smaller circles (fewer than 30 people), facilitation from your seat is usually adequate.

The **three primary types of cues** are

Grouping (who)

Action (what & when)

Dynamic (how)

(●) Grouping Cues

Before cueing a change within the circle, you must first identify what is to be changed. We do this by *grouping*. Grouping is a technique that allows you to specify which participants will be the subject of an action or dynamic cue. Grouping by location (a section of the circle, the "outer" circle, etc.) and grouping by traits (technique, pitch, timbre, etc.) are the two most common ways groups are defined.

Grouping by Location (where)

The whole circle.

A quarter section (arc).

To group an arc of the physical circle, first decide on the span of the arc (half, quarter, etc.).

1. Point to the edge of the arc with your hand (photo A).

2. Include all members of the arc by sweeping your hand from edge to edge as if to say,
   "All of you from here to there."

3. Define the edges of the arc with both your hands at the same time (photo B).

Tip: Point to the instruments instead of pointing at people. Pointing straight at a person is considered by some to be rude and may leave people feeling uncomfortable. It may also help to gesture with your hand rather than with your finger.

A **small arc** in DCMI:

Grouping by Traits (what)

All the drums.

All the shakers.

Three Ways of Grouping by Timbre

- Hold up a sample of the instrument group (such as a shaker to indicate all shakers) and point to it.

- Make the playing motions of an instrument group (such as shaking a shaker).

- Point to the instruments of participants who are playing from the chosen group.

All the shaken sounds in DCMI:

Some trait groups include:

- Instrument categories (hand-held, unpitched or pitched percussion)

- Instrument types (conga, tambourine, woodblock, cabasa)

- Instrument playing technique (hands, sticks, scraped)

- People traits (female/male, adults/children, a single person, wearing glasses, left-handed, born in July)

- Colors (Rainbow drums, Joia or Boomwhackers® percussion tubes, clothing worn)

Tip: Be sensitive when defining different groups within the circle. Once I was in Oakland playing with about 60 other people and the facilitator grouped "All the 49er fans!" to play. That poor guy was left playing all by himself!

Action Cues

Action cues provide the group with information about what you would like them to do and are essential for drum circle facilitation. These include starting, stopping, letting players know to continue playing and other actions such as *rumbling*. Action cues allow you to create segues and settings that help everyone play together, and they focus the group's attention and make for interesting music.

Play ▷

There are several ways to signal the group to start playing:

- Play a steady beat on an instrument and have the participants join you as they wish. (I like bells and tambourines for this.)

- Count off: "1, 2, Rea-dy, Play!"

- Ask the question, "Who's got the groove?" and let someone take the group into rhythm.

- Invite everyone to play a note each time you step (matching you), and increase the tempo of your steps until you're walking at a steady beat and the group is playing with you.

Stop

Stopping the group is easy when you set your cue and make clear motions. Here are some ways to give a group a stop cue:

- Cross your hands in front of your chest (photo 1A) and swing them out quickly, like an umpire's motion for "safe" in baseball (photo 1B).

1A   **1B**

- Hold up your arm, hand in fist (photo 2A) and bring it down quickly to your side, like the motion for "*Yes!*" or "*Cha-Ching!*" (photo 2B).

- Step to the rhythm (matching the group), and slow down until everyone is playing right with your footsteps, then end with one big step. (This is the reverse version of starting the group by stepping.)

 **Continue**

To cue a group to continue playing, first define the group you are addressing. Then, make a rolling motion with one or both hands to signal, "Continue playing. Don't stop."

Note: In DCMI, continue may also be applied to the facilitator, as in, "Continue in a similar fashion."

 Rumble

A rumble happens when the members of the group are all playing a free-roll (not in time to the pulse).

To create a rumble, shake your hands or pretend you are playing a drum really fast, then raise your arms to encourage everyone to join in.

Dynamic Cues

Dynamic cues are used to modify action. You can use them to raise or lower the overall volume, increase or decrease the tempo of the music or produce accents. Changing the dynamics helps add variety and depth to the music by emphasizing and/or de-emphasizing certain elements.

⬆ **Volume Up**

To raise the volume, hold your arms out with palms facing up, and then make a lifting motion with your arms.

Tip: Sometimes I pretend I'm pressing something up over my head as though to say, "Push it up!"

 Volume Down

To lower the volume, hold your arms out with palms facing down, and then lower your arms as if saying, "Push it down."

Tip: Sometimes I motion as if I'm playing with my fingers only to give the idea of playing softly.

Tempo Up

To speed up the tempo, first give a "thumbs up" sign to indicate the tempo will be speeding up. Then, play an instrument or use large movements to match the group's tempo, and gradually speed up at a rate the participants can follow.

Tip: I often make exaggerated movements, even stepping along with the pulse, to provide a visual guide.

 ### Tempo Down

To slow down the tempo, first give a "thumbs down" sign to indicate the tempo will be slowing down. Then, match the group's tempo as you play or step to a steady beat, and become slower and slower until the group moves with you.

Walking around the inside of the circle, taking larger and larger steps, is very effective for slowing the tempo. I sometimes pretend I'm getting tired, losing energy, and take longer to get to the next beat. Slowing the tempo can be a very dramatic way to focus the group and segue into a new setting.

Tip: Another way to slow down is to speed up. That's right! If you speed up enough, participants will often end up subdividing or simplifying their rhythms so the net result is a groove that feels slower (a *half-time feel*). It's like shifting to a higher gear on a bicycle—your speed may be faster, but your pedaling is slower.

Accent

Here are two ways to emphasize specific notes or beats:

- Clap your hands.
- Make hand gestures, as if you are playing a drum.
- Mark beats with your footsteps.

Combination Cues

 ### Wave

A wave is a rumble that moves from one side of the circle to the other. It's a combination of grouping, volume up and volume down.

1. Create a rumble.
2. Lower the volume of the entire circle.
3. Group the circle in halves and raise the volume of one half with one hand while motioning for the other half to stay at a low volume with the other hand.
4. Alternate the volume of the two halves by moving your arms up and down in opposite directions using a see-saw motion.

A **wave** in a DCMI★ (text descriptions are provided for reference):

Circle : rumbles

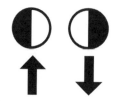
Circle: volume down

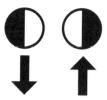
Half A: volume up / Half B: stay low

Half A: volume down / Half B: volume up

Making waves at the 2002 Percussive Arts Society International Convention.

 Orbit

Something is orbiting when it is moving around the edge of the circle.

You can create an *orbit rumble* by combining the rumble and stop cues:

1. With everyone resting, group a small arc of the circle to rumble.

2. Slowly, start to move the rumble around the circle by motioning for the participants who are next to the rumbling arc to start rumbling.

3. The same moment you start the next group, motion for the first group to stop.

Once the participants see the pattern, you can orbit the rumble around faster and even change directions.

An **orbit rumble** in DCMI:

Small arc 1: rumble

Small arc 2: rumble / Small arc 1: stop

Continue around circle

HAIKU

Hands play together
Waves of rhythm move through us
As we become one

★ *DCMI cues are often represented in pairs: a subject (top), paired with an action (bottom).*

Focus Cues

Listen to the Pulse

You can bring attention to the pulse by holding one hand to your ear and marking the pulse with the other (patting your chest, for example).

Listen to Them

Bring attention to a person or group by gesturing towards them. *(Remember to use your hand instead of pointing.)*

Chapter 5

 **Drum Circle Activities**

In this section, you'll learn how to use your facilitation techniques to create various settings and segues for your groups. In many cases, both verbal and non-verbal ways of achieving the same result are given. All the examples are summarized using DCMI, which may make them easier to learn. These are only a few examples of how you can create various settings; ultimately, you will create your own versions of these and design new settings, segues and cues that reflect your unique style.

Adding Timbre Groups

Non-Verbal Approach

1. Hold up a member of a specific timbre group, such as shakers. Cue that group to continue playing.

2. Stop the rest of the group while the shakers continue.

3. Add the wood sounds by motioning for them to start playing (as if playing a woodblock).

4. Add the bells (metal) sounds (as if playing a triangle).

5. Add the drums (as if playing a drum).

Verbal Approach

1. Set a stop cue.

2. On the downbeat of the stop, say twice in rhythm, "All–the–sha-kers, Come–on–in."

3. Have the group listen to the shakers.

4. When ready, say, "All the wood sounds, come on in."

5. When ready, say, "All the bells, come on in."

6. To finish, say, "All the drums, come on in," or "Everybody else, come on in."

Adding Timbre Groups in DCMI:

| Shakers: continue | Circle: stop | Wood sounds: play | Metal sounds: play | Drums: play |

Groove & Echo

1. Cue half the circle to continue playing. Set a stop cue for the other half of the circle. Stop the section and motion for them to listen to the rest of the group.

2. Choose a loud instrument such as a cowbell or woodblock. Set the echo by pointing to yourself, then to the listening group. Play a short phrase that ends on a strong beat.

3. Motion to the listening group to echo you. Continue echoes with the group while the rest of the circle plays.

4. When ready to segue the echo group back to the groove, use a verbal cue such as "1–2, Make-up-your-own!" or "Everybody keep on playing." Support the verbal cue with a "continue playing" motion.

Groove & Echo in DCMI:

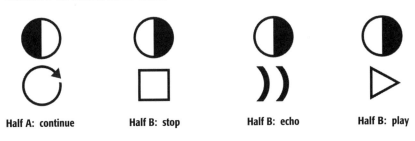

| Half A: continue | Half B: stop | Half B: echo | Half B: play |

To Voices and Back

1. Set an echo cue and point to your mouth to let them know they are going to be vocalizing. Stop the group and chant a short pattern such as this one:

1	+	2	+	3	+	4	+
Huh			Ha		Yeh	Yeh	

2. While you're vocalizing, motion for the group to echo you with their voices (point to your smile). Continue vocalizing different chants for the group to echo.

3. Repeat the same vocal pattern a few times and motion for one section (1/4 arc, for example) to continue the pattern on their own (without resting).

4. Have other sections chant complementary patterns to create a circle of vocal grooves.

5. Ask the participants to offer new patterns.

6. Reflect new parts back to the different sections. (Remember to rotate to each section so they don't get stuck on one phrase for too long.)

7. When ready, set and cue everyone (all at once or in sections) to "play what you say" and move the vocals onto the instruments.

To Voices and Back in DCMI:

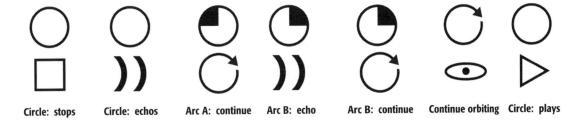

| Circle: stops | Circle: echos | Arc A: continue | Arc B: echo | Arc B: continue | Continue orbiting | Circle: plays |

Note to Music Educators

Be sure to encourage your students to learn the art of facilitation by talking with them about the DCM philosophy and techniques and by helping them apply the technology to create their own music. Allow time for those who wish to step into the circle and work with their peers. You also might encourage students to facilitate music making during a family night or assembly. Have them learn DCMI, create their own activities, and transcribe one another's facilitation.

Imagine how the world could change if more people became facilitators of creativity and expression. It all starts with our children.

HAIKU
This is how we learn
Listening and echoing
Now we can say more

Orbit Echo

1. Set and cue the group to echo you in rhythm several times.

2. As the group is echoing one of your patterns, choose someone from the group to take the lead. Point to that person's instrument to let everyone know this is the new leader. Sometimes it takes a couple of phrases before a new leader realizes that he or she has been chosen. If the new leader doesn't play anything, that's ok—you can always have the group echo silence!

3 Continue until the group sees that the new pattern and leadership is being orbited around the circle.

4. Segue the group into a new setting when ready.

Orbit Echo in DCMI:

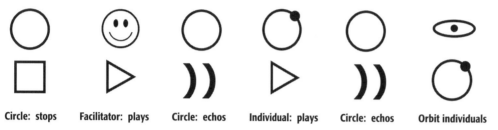

Circle: stops   Facilitator: plays   Circle: echos   Individual: plays   Circle: echos   Orbit individuals

Option: Have the next leader be the only one to echo as the group pats or snaps the pulse.

Orbit Answer

1. Play a specific pattern several times (this is the question phrase), and have the group echo you.

2. Motion for the group to continue playing the question phrase, leaving a space of equal length (the space in which you were playing) after each time they play.

3. Once the pattern of playing and resting is established, begin to riff (play an answer) when the group is resting. If they start to echo you, remind them that their role is to continue playing the same question.

4. Pass the lead to a member of the circle, having them answer the group in the space.

5. Orbit the lead around the circle. Segue the group into a new setting when ready.

Orbit Answer in DCMI:

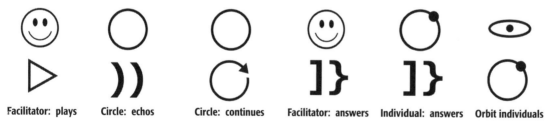

Facilitator: plays   Circle: echos   Circle: continues   Facilitator: answers   Individual: answers   Orbit individuals

Note: Orbit games are best-suited for small to medium-size groups (10 to 30 people). When considering presenting an orbit game, take into account how long it may take for everyone to have a turn.

Groove Pass

1. Group a quarter of the circle and cue them to continue playing.

2. Set and cue the rest of the circle to stop, and listen to the players.

3. Cue a quarter of the circle adjacent to the players to be ready (as in setting a cue).

4. Set a stop for the players by counting down, "4–3–2–1, *Stop.*" On the stop cue, start the next group at the same time by "passing the groove" to them.

5. Continue passing the groove around the circle.
   Option: Create phrases of fixed length, such as 8 beats, so players will know when to play and rest. Shorten phrases until each section is playing only 4 or 2 beats of the groove before passing it on.

6. Segue into a rumble by speeding up until all sections are playing at once!

Groove Pass in DCMI:

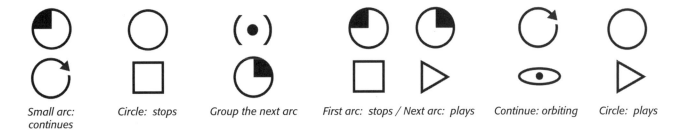

| Small arc: continues | Circle: stops | Group the next arc | First arc: stops / Next arc: plays | Continue: orbiting | Circle: plays |

Note: Facilitation involves much more than simply using cues to lead the group through pre-planned activities. It's fine to have a "box of facilitation tricks" handy, but keep in mind that climbing too deep into your box can prevent you from seeing the ideas that are coming from the participants—in the moment. Using facilitation cues to provide a variety of settings for your group can make an event fun and interesting, but it's important to observe the group as well and be ready to follow them down their own musical path at a moment's notice.

We Are All Children

I was presenting a drum circle at a family night for a K–8 school in Southern California. I brought instruments for about 60 people and had set up in the multi-purpose room. When it was time for the circle to start, children and their parents were ushered into the room. The children immediately ran to the instruments and started to explore them, trying out different ones to see what they sounded like and forgetting themselves in the moment. I was very happy to see them enjoying themselves. Something seemed to be missing, however.

Where were the parents? I looked around and was quite surprised to see that most, if not all, of the adults seemed to be glued to the walls! They came in with their children, sending them over to the music area while they stood watching like statues. It took me about ten minutes to unglue the adults and get them involved in the music. Once they joined in, they all had a great time, but it seemed as if most of the grown-ups viewed music as "something that children do." Many of them lacked the curiosity and I-don't-care-who's-watching-ness of the children. It was as if they were embarrassed to try playing music with their children.

Perhaps they were worried about sounding bad or making mistakes. Maybe they had been told that they don't have musical talent or had negative performance experiences when they were young. Who knows. What I do know is that the belief that "music for fun is only for children" is a problem for our society.

How do we change that belief?

We do it by sharing our creative spirit.

We do it by helping everyone remember that we are all children.

We do it one circle at a time.

Chapter 6

 Presenting a Drum Circle

The following information will help you organize, plan and present a community-style drum circle for your family, friends, business, organization, or the general public. For information about how to present and facilitate rhythm-based events for specific populations such as children or training purposes, see "Specific Populations" on page 66.

Preparation

Find a Location

Choose a venue that is large enough for your expected number of participants to gather in a circle, with some room to spare. It should be open and free of obstacles such as pillars so that everyone can see one another and the facilitator.

Consider the following:

Are there sufficient chairs and tables available?

Are there noise restrictions?

Is there ample parking?

Are there restrooms nearby?

Will you be making refreshments available?

Will people be able to easily find the room?

Is there easy access for loading gear in and out?

Is there wheelchair access?

Note: Possible venues include music stores, recreation centers, churches, and schools.

Identify Your Team

The Facilitator (That's you.)

The Coordinator works with the facilitator and venue to arrange, promote and present the event. (This could be you.)

The Host is someone who represents the venue, or host group. (This could still be you.)

The Crew helps set up chairs and tables, load in gear, etc. (Hopefully not just you.)

The Greeters welcome the participants, make sure everyone knows where to go and what to do when they arrive. (If this is still you, it's time you learn how to ask for help!)

Set a Date & Time

Decide when to hold your event. Make sure you give yourself plenty of time to get the word out and that all the members of your team can be there. Most drums circles run from one to two hours (educational or special-event drum circles may be shorter). If your event is not where your drums are, allow at least one hour before and after your event for setting up and packing up.

Promote Your Event

Get the word out early. If possible, send out e-mails, flyers and postings at least six weeks prior to your event. Follow up with reminders two weeks before and then a few days before your event.

Promote via the Internet, e-mail lists, websites (RecreationalMusic.com, for example) and list-serves. Local papers also run free community event listings. In addition to date, location and time, include some of the following information in your message:

Enjoy making group music!

No experience necessary.

Bring your drum or use one of ours.

Have fun playing hand drums.

Facilitated by *(facilitator)*.

Tip: Planning forms, event checklists, coordinator guides, directional signs and other helpful resources are available at **drumcirclemusic.com**.

Gather Your Instruments

Put together a mixture of instruments. Use the guide on page 94 to build a kit that is right for the size and demographics of your group.

If transporting your instruments, use different colored bags to store and transport the hand-held percussion and sticks:

- Metal sounds (a mixture of bells, tambourines, triangles and finger cymbals)

- Wood sounds (tone and woodblocks, frogs, and clappers)

- Shakers, rattles and scrapers (axatse, cabasas, guiros, shékeres, etc.)

- Various sticks, mallets, beaters, and miscellaneous items, such as tuning keys & wrenches

Tip: By placing similar items together, you not only make it easy to find specific items, but you reduce the damage that can be caused when metal instruments knock against the more delicate shakers and rattles.

Place your four bags (and other items such as nesting frame drums) into one medium-size plastic case. With the addition of a few larger drums (bass drums, congas, jembes, etc.), this kit will easily provide enough instruments for most drum circles. Plastic storage bins also work well for hand-held percussion instruments and sticks. Organizing the instruments this way will allow you to quickly find and distribute instruments and makes putting them away fast and easy.

Tip: When moving your drums, always take care to pack them well, and use cases, or at least packing blankets, to protect them while in transport.

Setting the Circle

The Physical Circle

Decide where the center of your circle will be and set up your chairs around it, leaving two or three openings for people to enter and exit. Set up chairs according to how many people you expect. Armless chairs are preferred as they provide more elbowroom for drumming.

For circles of up to 30 people, setting a single row of chairs works well.

For circles with more than 30 people, you have two options:

1. Provide chairs for everyone by arranging them in concentric circles. Leave enough space between rows for people to play a drum and still move around.

2. Form a *rhythm riser* (concentric circles of graduated height). This helps maintain the lines of sight between participants because no one is looking at the back of someone's head.

Setting up a rhythm riser is easy. Set up one row of chairs for about one third of your participants (those playing "sit down" drums). Invite some participants who have hand-held instruments to form an outer circle around the chairs. Create an inner circle of people sitting on the floor.

Tip: Create a multi-generational rhythm riser by grouping children in the inner circle with their parents seated in chairs behind them.

Why a Circle?

We gather in a circle because it allows the participants to see one another, permits everyone to hear each other in a balanced setting, provides a sense of inclusion and equity, and helps everyone to feel they are valued and important.

Circles can represent many things to many people:

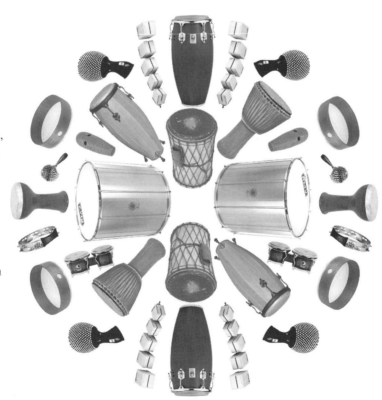

- the perfect form, stability, oneness

- the Sun, Earth, and Moon and their orbits

- the Canopy of the heavens

- a wheel and motion

- the womb

- ripples in a pond

- the limitless, eternity, the absolute

- enlightenment

- a labyrinth or mandala

A drum circle is a mandala of sound.

Providing the Instruments

You can make the instruments available to participants in the following ways:

- Place instruments at each chair before the participants arrive.

- Offer instruments outside the circle by placing them on tables or in a designated area, allowing participants to choose an instrument as they enter the circle.

- Use a combination of the above by placing large drums in the circle and offering small percussion instruments outside.

Tip: For those bringing their own instruments (in addition to using yours), provide tags or stickers at the door so participants can mark their personal instruments in order to avoid confusion at the end of the event.

The population with whom you are working may determine which of these options is best for your event. If you're working with children, for example, you may want to organize the instruments beforehand (option 1, above) to keep your program running smoothly. If you are working with a group in a training exercise, you may wish to allow your participants to choose their own instruments (option 2, above).

Arranging the Instruments

Unlike an orchestra, there is no set format for arranging the instruments in a drum circle. There are, however, some things you can do to make it easier for everyone to play together:

- In a multi-row circle or rhythm riser, place the loud instruments (bass drums, cowbells, woodblocks) on the inside circle. This helps everyone feel the pulse. If you are using more than one bass drum, position them across from each other to balance the sound levels.

- Place similar instruments in pairs or small groups. It's helpful for some people to have a "rhythm buddy" with whom they can play.

- Provide various sticks and mallets. These come in handy for reducing the volume levels of the louder instruments such as woodblocks and cowbells, and can also be used on hand drums such as congas and bongos to give people's hands a rest. See page 103 for more information on the Kalani Drum Circle Signature Line.

Circle Stick, Hand Drumming Glove, Dundun Stick, Handtone, Circle Mallets

Signs & Information

- Set out information and flyers for other events, services, etc., on a table near the entrance.

- If needed, place directional signs [**Drum Circle ➡**] from the parking area to the location. You may wish to provide signs pointing to the restrooms as well.

- Designate an area for people to place personal items, coats, bags, etc.

- Have a sign-in sheet or a place for people to leave their business cards so they can be notified about future events (or to sign up for a door prize).

- Have 3x5 cards or evaluation forms available so you can get feedback from the participants.

OK—now the fun begins. You've done all your homework, now it's time to play!

Inclusion

Welcome to Your Drum Circle

Some people may have never been to a drum circle before, so they will be looking for some direction about where to sit, what the instruments are, what to do when they find a place in the circle, and so on. You can always spot these folks because they are excited to be there, but often have looks on their faces that are similar to a child who is showing up for his first day of school: he's ready to play, but not sure what to do or how to fit in. Call your greeters into action! By welcoming people into your circle, you let them know that their presence is appreciated.

The **role of a greeter** is to welcome people to the event, point out the information table, help everyone choose an instrument, and encourage participants to join the circle and start playing. The role of the greeter continues even after the circle has begun, as they welcome latecomers into the circle and address the needs of the participants throughout the event.

Note: For children's circles, it's best to have more structure. For example, you may choose to bring them in as a group (as if coming from their classroom).

Let's Drum!

If people are not playing already, provide a simple warm-up rhythm to get the drumming started and invite everyone to join you. You can also ask someone else to take the lead and bring the group into rhythm. I often invite those who come early to "play some welcoming music" for people as they join the circle. This helps set the tone and involves everyone right from the start.

It's always a good idea to encourage people to warm up a bit before starting to play hand drums. This includes taking time to stretch the fingers, hands and arms, and find a comfortable drumming position. If possible, add a warm-up to your inclusion segment as a way to help them feel comfortable with their instruments and ease them into their music.

> **Tip:** Suggest that participants "shake hands" (shake hands in the air) as a group to help them loosen up, relax, and connect with one another. Have them wave "hello" to the people around and across from them. Starting off with a short body percussion activity is also a good way to help people warm up their hands before moving to the hand drums.

Provide people with a sense of inclusion:

- Give technical help to those who need it.
- Make sure everyone has an instrument they are comfortable playing.
- Encourage participation by inviting everyone to join the circle.
- Make it a point to greet everyone with your eyes and a smile.

Formally welcome everyone into the circle.

After a few minutes of drumming together, you and/or the host may wish to make a few announcements:

- Welcome and thank everyone for coming.
- Introduce and thank the host, coordinator and facilitator.
- Encourage everyone to greet each other.

Provide drum circle etiquette guidelines:

- Remove rings, bracelets and watches when playing hand drums.
- Be conscientious of the volume.
- Parents look after their children.
- Ask before playing someone else's drum.

Why talk about the guidelines when you can SING about them?

Most participants prefer being actively involved to passively sitting by while you recite a bunch of "drum circle rules." Here's a fun way you can provide some drum circle guidelines and involve everyone at the same time:

1. Tell everyone that there are some guidelines that we follow when we drum together.

2. Explain that you will let them know what they are, but that you need them to help you.

3. Start by singing the following phrases to the melody "She'll Be Comin' 'Round the Mountain."

> We'll be *listening to each other* when we drum…
> We'll be *listening to each other* when we drum…
> We'll be listening to each other,
> We'll be listening to each other,
> We'll be *listening to each other* when we **drum**…
> (Give them the next line to the song in this space, starting on the word **drum** of the last line.)

Other possible lines:

> *…lookin' across the circle…*
> *…making our own rhythms…*
> *…conscious of the volume…*
> *…playing for each other…*

Add your line(s) here:

_____

_____

_____

Cooperation

Once everyone has found a place in the circle and announcements have been made, continue with the body of your program. (The majority of the activities will take place during this phase in your event.)

- Use your facilitation skills to guide the group through various settings.
- Facilitate music and/or games that are appropriate for the specific type of circle (e.g., community, educational, training, etc.).
- Rely on your intuition to strike a balance between leading and following.

Appreciation

When you are ready to bring the circle to a close,

- direct the focus of the activities to those of connection and community;
- acknowledge each other's gifts and contributions;
- provide time for personal reflection and/or group affirmations;
- close the circle with a sense of gratitude.

Tip: Use the Inclusion, Cooperation and Appreciation Strategies outlined in the chapter Philosophy and Approach on page 18.

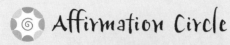

Affirmation Circle

This is a fun activity that provides participants with the opportunity to celebrate their experience by making positive statements within a musical setting.

1. Establish a pattern through matching or echoing in which everyone repeats an 8-beat pattern, playing for 6 beats, stopping together on beat 7, and resting on beat 8.

2. On beat 8, boldly state a word that reflects the spirit or message of the circle, for example, *rhythm, joy, peace, love, light, spirit, fun,* or *freedom.*

3. Continue the pattern and orbit statements around the circle so everyone has an opportunity to contribute.

1	2	3	4	5	6	7	8
Play	Play	Play	Play	Play	Play	Stop	[statement]

This is a nice way to end the circle and allows participants to share their thoughts and express their feelings without having to make speeches. Allow for non-verbal or musical statements as well as spoken ones. (This activity is a bit like Orbit Answer on page 40, but uses words.)

After the Circle

Stay in the Groove

The rhythm doesn't end when the music stops. Keep the spirit of the circle alive:

- Invite the participants to share their experiences with you by filling out comment cards.
- Offer information about future events through flyers.
- Ask participants to join your mailing list.
- Ask participants to invite a friend to the next event.

Tip: Keep a journal of your experiences and/or share your message through the Drum Circle Music list (send an e-mail to DrumCircleMusic-subscribe@yahoogroups.com to join).

Celebrate

Take your team out to dinner.

Great job!

Chapter 7

 # Tuning the Circle

As you work with a variety of groups, you will experience many different forms of a drum circle. Some will take place in small rooms with low ceilings, others will be outside under the endless sky. Some may have ten people and others will have hundreds. Keeping your circle intact involves skills and techniques that extend beyond the basic drum circle facilitation tools you've learned so far. Every system can break down in certain areas and may need a little tuning from time to time. This is a natural process and can offer both mental and emotional challenges. Finding ways to incorporate some effective and relatively transparent drum circle Feng Shui is part of becoming a Drum Circle Music facilitator.

The Three-Fold Circle

A drum circle is really three circles in one:

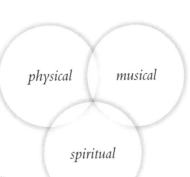

The physical circle

The circle of music

The circle of spirit

It is in caring for all three that we effectively facilitate group music making.

The Physical Circle

KEY CONCEPTS
Accessibility • Equity • Flexibility

As an event unfolds, the circle can change shape as participants come and go, move around, and interact. Rearranging, adding, or removing chairs is one way to accommodate these changes.

If there are more chairs than people, remove some chairs and make the circle smaller or have people move to the inner rows of a multi-row circle.

If participants have bunched up on one side of the circle, wait for an appropriate moment such as a natural break in the music, then ask them if they could work together to make their spacing more even.

If you have more people than expected, add chairs or start a rhythm riser. Offer a movement activity that can take place in the center of the circle.

> **Tip:** In order to create a more intimate setting, you might want to ask people to form a rhythm riser even if there are enough chairs.

Of course, the ultimate goal is to provide a rich and rewarding experience for the participants, not to force them to constantly shift their seats to maintain a perfect circle. Use your judgment to determine if the physical circle is in need of tuning. If it's working for the participants, let it be a drum square, half-circle, triangle or whatever it wants to be. The circles of *music* and *spirit* always take precedence over the physical circle.

HAIKU
Sight is blocked by heads
Create a Rhythm Riser
Now we see faces

 **The Circle of Music**

KEY CONCEPTS
Simple • Guidance • Options

Drum circles are social events that take place in musical settings. Because the playing of drums and percussion instruments is the common vehicle for group (and individual) expression, we must do our best to help everyone create musical successes and feel the joys of being together in rhythm. As I mentioned at the beginning of this book, a drum circle is not a drum class; therefore, it's important to remember to always meet the group where *they are*, and not try too hard to push them to where *you think* they should be. There are, however, some simple strategies you can use to help them make the best possible music. Below are various options you can use to help everyone play together.

If the tempo seems to be dragging (slowing down):

- Play a steady beat on a supportive instrument such as a bell or bass drum.
- Mark the pulse by stepping or patting your chest as if to say, "Let's all feel the beat."
- Go with the change and steady it at a slower tempo.
- Let the pace slow down until the groove ends on its own, then segue into a new setting.

If the tempo is speeding up:

- Play a steady beat on a supportive instrument such as a bell or bass drum.
- Mark the pulse by stepping or patting your chest as if to say, "Let's all feel the beat."
- Speed up until the groove subdivides naturally and steady it at that tempo.
- Play subdivisions of the beat to connect the space between notes.
- Speed up until a natural rumble occurs, then segue into a new setting.

If the volume is too loud:

- Lower the volume of the entire group.
- Provide alternative sticks and mallets for people playing loud instruments.
- Segue into a setting that involves resting such as orbit, groove pass, or groove & echo.

When Is the Volume Too Loud?

- When you have to shout in someone's ear to be heard.
- When you can't hear the people across the circle from you.
- When the over-all volume of the circle is over 85dB. (A blow dryer is about 105dB.)

Health Tip: It's a good idea to protect your hearing by using ear plugs; however, participants who use ear plugs may be inclined to play at levels that are too loud for those who are not wearing them. Unless *everyone* in the circle is using ear protection, it may be a better idea to ask everyone to simply play softer or use alternative sticks and mallets to produce lower sound levels, rather than putting some people's hearing at risk.

If the group constantly speeds up, encourage a body percussion activity that uses gross motor skills such as stepping or large arm movements to help participants feel the pulse. This also limits the amount of speeding up that can occur by tying the steady beat to a movement that is difficult to do quickly.

Offer a way for the participants to subdivide the pulse (divide it into many smaller, equal segments) thereby creating a *rhythmic grid* they can align with. For example, you might suggest they say the word "Chattanooga," either to themselves or out loud, as they play the beat. This may help keep the group stay at an even tempo because it becomes difficult to say at faster tempos. (See "The Groove" on page 29 for more options.)

If the group has trouble keeping a steady beat, play the pulse on a supportive instrument like a bell or bass drum. Try an echo activity such as groove & echo (p. 38) or orbit echo (p. 40).

Focus on activities or games that do not require the group to stay in rhythm such as rumble ball (p. 60), or tell a story and have the participants make up the soundtrack (a *sound scape*).

Encourage a body percussion activity that uses gross motor skills such as stepping or large arm movements. This will help everyone feel the pulse in their bodies and may translate to the instruments.

Use a familiar song to help stay in rhythm:

1. Recite a familiar tune with the group such as the "Alphabet Song."
2. Step to the words and say them.
3. Step to the song without saying the words.
4. "Play" the rhythm of the song on the instruments.
5. Have half of the group start eight beats after the other half begins (as in a *round*).
6. Try different combinations of the above in a sequence (say, step, clap, play, etc.).

The Circle of Spirit

KEY CONCEPTS
Acceptance • Space • Resiliency

The opportunity to serve a group of people is a gift. To be called upon to help others come together in rhythm is a magical and precious thing. Whenever I witness a moment of growth or epiphany in a circle, it lifts my spirit and feeds my soul. But there are some aspects of facilitation that can cause unnecessary anxiety.

As we are often in a position of leadership, we may find ourselves believing that we are responsible for certain outcomes in the circle such as the following:

- Keeping the rhythm together
- Making sure that everyone is having a good time
- Keeping the group's energy level at a high point

Naturally, it feels great when the rhythm stays together and everyone is having the time of their lives, but are these outcomes that you can guarantee? Not at all. The facilitator's role is to help maximize the chances for success, not to force an outcome by making sure the players don't lose the beat, or by acting the clown just to get them to smile. I'm not sure if these tendencies come from our own need to be in the spotlight, to be in control or to be liked by everyone, but there are bound to be times when the rhythm will fall apart, someone will not have a good time, or the group's energy will run low.

- If the rhythm falls apart, let it—and then help the group understand why.
- If someone isn't connecting with the group, allow them the space to connect with themselves.
- If the energy level isn't where you think it should be, go where it is—and go deeper.

By letting go of expectations and focusing on the process of improvisation and discovery, we become part of the circle of spirit and allow ourselves the freedom to experience the circle as a participant.

While *what* happens in the circle is not the responsibility of the facilitator, *how* it happens is.

Aligning the Three-Fold Circle

KEY CONCEPTS
Structure • Observation • Dynamics

An Example of a Dissonant Circle

I was attending a major convention where an evening drum circle was taking place. As I entered the room, I immediately noticed that there were two groups of people in the room: those who were *in* the circle and those who were *watching* the circle. Upon further observation, it became clear why:

- The circle that had been set up was too small to accommodate newcomers.

- There were not sufficient openings for people to enter the circle.

- There were not enough instruments for everyone.

- The facilitator could not see who was coming into the room because he had his back to the door.

- The facilitator was leading a *drum-class* style circle by passing out specific parts for people to learn and perform.

- Many of the participants were overwhelmed with the technical difficulty of the music.

- There were no greeters.

- People were entering, then leaving the room because it seemed as if there was no place for them.

By applying the Drum Circle Music concept of tuning the three-fold circle, the facilitator could help this group to reach higher levels of inclusion, cooperation and appreciation:

The Physical Circle

- Add chairs and expand the circle to accommodate newcomers.

- Provide more instruments.

- Make sure there is at least one greeter to welcome people into the circle.

- Create openings in the circle for people to enter.

- Face the facilitator towards the door so he can see newcomers and welcome them into the circle.

The Circle of Music

- Provide body percussion activities to include those with only their "original" instruments.

- Rotate the use of instruments so everyone gets a turn.

- Allow people to improvise, creating music that is right for them.

- Incorporate musical ideas from the participants.

- Help those who need and ask for assistance with technique or other issues.

The Circle of Spirit

- By creating space in the circle for everyone, participants feel included.

- Providing everyone with an instrument, or at least a way to be musically involved, makes them feel valued.

- When people are allowed to improvise and express their own music, the circle becomes theirs.

- By helping those who need it, the facilitator empowers people to become productive members of the musical community, boosting the potential and spirit of the entire circle.

- By acknowledging people's contributions, they feel appreciated.

As you may conclude from the example of the Dissonant Circle, the state of the spiritual circle depends largely on the state of the physical and musical circles. By providing participants with an environment that supports them, offering musical tools they can use, and providing opportunities for cooperation, any circle can become a high-functioning atmosphere where everyone feels included, supported and appreciated.

It is when we facilitate the structure and functionality of the three-fold circle that we provide our participants with the best experience possible. The ability to create, observe and understand the dynamics of these three interdependent elements, bringing them into a cohesive experience, is perhaps the most important skill a facilitator can have.

Personal Connections

Most of the time, drum circle participants are eager to play their instruments and work together to create the best possible outcome. What happens, though, when people aren't sure they're ready to jump into the circle (the *Reluctant Participant*), are out of sync with the group (the *Oblivious Distracter*), or are just not cooperative (the *Rebel*)? Sometimes our facilitation skills require that we move from the area of music facilitation to the more personal area of *people management*. There are ways to turn potentially disruptive actions into positive experiences without shattering egos or detracting from the experience. Next, we look at three types of participants and several ways to help them connect with the group in productive and appropriate ways.

The Reluctant Participant

KEY CONCEPTS
Acceptance • Options • Support

> *Happiness often sneaks through a door you didn't know you left open.*
>
> **—Mildred Barthel**

Sometimes participants are not sure how to fit into a drum circle setting. They may have arrived after the inclusion segment and feel like an outsider, not wanting to disrupt the flow of the activity; they could be experiencing their first drum circle, feeling a little overwhelmed with all the activity; or they could just be curious and want to watch everyone play for a while and listen to the music. Reluctant participants can usually be seen sitting a "safe" distance from the circle or standing against a wall. More often than not, these participants *want* to join the circle, but they're not sure what to do. Here are a few ways you can help the reluctant participant feel at home in your circle:

- Acknowledge their presence, letting them know that it's OK to be where they are. Don't risk making them feel even more like outsiders by pointing out that they're not participating. Give them permission not to participate, but let them know they are part of the group.

- Bring them an instrument. They may say, "No thanks—I'm just here to listen." That's fine. Place it on a nearby chair and say, "Just in case you change your mind." (They usually do.)

- Wait for a natural opening in the music and make an announcement that "we have some new people to welcome into the circle." Segue into an activity that allows anyone wishing to join the circle to become an active participant. Rearrange chairs if necessary to facilitate the inclusion of the newcomers.

The Oblivious Distracter

KEY CONCEPTS
Alternatives • Flexibility • Creativity

As much as we may believe that we are all musical, and that we need and deserve to be heard and to express ourselves, sometimes the "joyful noise" of one person may simply be "noise" to another or even to the entire circle. On some occasions, even the power of *entrainment* (traveling the same speed, as aboard a train) seems to leave someone stranded at the station platform, beating out rhythms that appear to be coming from another train on a different track or even in another time zone! This is part of what a drum circle can illustrate—namely, that not everyone hears the same rhythms in the same ways, and that we are all at different points along our musical and rhythmic paths. When the rhythm of the group is being intersected in such a way that it throws some participants out of sync, it can produce not only musical tension (which is not always a bad thing), but emotional tension as well. Some participants may start to "vibe" that person or play really loud in the hope that they will "get the message" and fall into the groove. Others will simply put up with it, but inside they may be fighting the urge to leave the circle or to try and stop the person from "ruining it" for them. Now the question becomes, "How do we help the group create a positive experience in this situation?" We can't take time to give someone music lessons on the spot, nor should we ask them to stop playing (which would only embarrass them and possibly turn them off to music making). The goal is always to help the group in the best possible way and to allow everyone to maximize their collective experience.

If someone's heart is in the right place, even though their rhythm is not, here are some ways you can support them and the group to produce a win-win outcome:

- Offer an instrument that plays a supportive role such as a shaker or rattle. These instruments contribute to the groove but do not carry as much musical weight as the bass drums, bells or wood sounds. It's best to do this in a way that is not too obvious. For example, you could choose several people to switch instruments at the same time so no one is singled out.

- Ask the person to match someone else in the circle (who is playing with the beat), thereby providing some rhythmic guidance.

- Segue into an echo activity to focus the group and create more space in the music.

Using scarves to make the music visual.

- Segue into a freeform exploration of sound (a.k.a. a *sound scape)* or a music game that focuses on aspects of music other than rhythm including timbre, dynamics and pitch (Rumble Ball, on page 60 is a good example).

- Tell a story and have the group play the soundtrack or mime an activity, and invite them to create sounds that match your movement. This allows everyone to participate in their own way without rhythmic requirements.

Tip: See *The Amazing Jamnasium* for more non-rhythmic activities.

HAIKU
Use different timbres
To make a story in sound
Take them on a trip

The Rebel

KEY CONCEPTS
Channeling • Entrainment • Teamwork

Sometimes people just don't feel like doing what everyone else is doing. That's OK, but unfortunately this desire to be different usually comes out as a rhythmic or musical rebellion. It could be one person or a whole section of people who are "into their own thing," making noise when the group is silent or listening to the facilitator or creating their own sub-grooves to pull the group in a different direction. As facilitators we may feel the need to confront or suppress these people, but if we understand what could be at the root of their behavior, perhaps we can help them and the group get back on track and spare everyone an unnecessary confrontation. Most rebels are driven by a need to show everyone else that "they are different," "can think for themselves" and they want to "make their mark." At the root of rebellion is a need for space and a fear of being limited. What they don't understand is that their behavior often leads to a lack of respect from others as they are looked upon as people who can't work with others and only care about themselves. Before you kick the rebels out of your circle, which may only add to their rebellious tendencies, try these win-win options:

- Give them a special role such as leading an echo activity or ask them to help you facilitate in some way. This will support their "need to lead" and give them the elevated status they are yearning for.

- Create space for the rebel and let them go nuts. If someone is in need of some attention, why not give it to them! They will be so thrilled that they'll dive into the spotlight and soon become tired of listening to themselves, just as flames that burn bright often burn quickly. At that point you can bring the group back in and the rebel will be happy they got to "do their thing." If they can actually play well and with good energy, listening to them play might be a nice treat for the other participants, and supply a good vibe that can be channeled back into the group.

- Go with them (entrainment). If they're pulling the groove in a different direction, go where they are taking it! This will support their need to "be different" while the group entrains with them. Of course as soon as the group is playing with them, they are no longer different!

- Let them know that it's OK to opt-out and not play. For example you could say: "If you feel like doing something else besides playing along, that's fine. You're welcome to wait until we're done with this, then you can come back when you're ready." Guess which option they are likely to choose!

Tip: When dealing with people who could be disruptive to the circle, for any reason, be discrete and do your best to keep their egos in tact by not publicly confronting or challenging them. We create community by building bridges, not by burning them.

The Drum Circle Debilitator

KEY CONCEPTS
Service • Humility • Guidance

> *Correction does much, but encouragement does more.*
>
> **—Johann Wolfgang von Goethe**

There are ways a facilitator can end up becoming a *debilitator*. I know because I, myself, have been one at times, and I've seen many others become one as well. Facilitation is a subtle art form, and we may—because of insecurity or lack of self-trust— find ourselves reaching for ineffective tools or falling into traps that are based on the need to feed our egos or control outcomes.

You may, at times, find yourself getting bored with the circle's music and decide to spice things up by having people play faster or more complicated rhythms, but this is not facilitation. Serving your own need to be entertained by having the group perform for you or anyone else is not only selfish, but it can also place unnecessary stress on many of the participants as they try to keep up with your pacing. One of the best things about a drum circle is that there is no audience! There is no ultimate standard upon which the music is being judged, and there is no pressure to perform. (That kind of pressure is why many people stop playing music in the first place.) The last thing you want to do as a facilitator is bring back someone's recital nightmares by putting them on the spot or having them jumping through musical hoops just to keep *you* entertained. Remember who you are working for, and help them play together as best they can.

**Playing drum,
not listening, etc.**

Signs of the Debilitator

- Uses the drum circle to showcase his or her own playing or "facilitation abilities."

- Runs the circle like a drum class, passing out specific parts and insists that everyone play them "correctly."

- Controls and limits the participants' input by forcing a personal agenda on the group.

- Tasks the group with patterns or tempos that are difficult for them to play comfortably.

- Continually conducts from the center of the circle, never joining the participants and playing along.

- Intimidates or challenges those who don't "get with the program."

- Has the time of his or her life and believes everyone else must feel the same way.

Recognizing these tendencies in your own facilitation is an important step in growing as a facilitator. Sometimes *not* facilitating is the best way you can serve the group.

Note: The terms "rebel" and "debilitator" identify behaviors, and not people. Care should be taken not to use them as "labels" for people, but as indicators of potential growth areas.

Getting to Know You: Applying the Theory of Multiple Intelligences

Being a good observer starts with looking and listening, but being able to recognize what we see and hear often requires a deeper level of training and awareness. For example, if someone in your circle seems to be disconnected from an activity, you might assume that they are simply tired; however, it is just as likely that they are feeling bored or even overwhelmed. How can you help the person if you don't know what they are feeling?

Developing a deeper understanding and awareness of personal and group dynamics requires that we first acknowledge that everyone in the world thinks, learns and communicates in different ways (hurray for that!) In his book *Frames of Mind: The Theory of Multiple Intelligences* (New York: BasicBooks, 1983), Howard Gardner presented the idea of *multiple intelligences*. His design of human learning styles and ways of thinking is comprised of at least eight separate but interconnected intelligences that, together, form the basis for a cross-cultural perspective of human cognition. Brief descriptions of these eight intelligences are discussed below, with examples of how each is used and ways they might be expressed by someone in musical terms.

To most effectively facilitate group creativity and expression, we must, on some level, also be facilitating individual experiences within the group. As a facilitator, my goal is to discover, through my own study and observation, how the participants in a given group express themselves and to provide activities and options that relate to their learning styles whether they be verbal, mathematical, visual, kinesthetic, musical, interpersonal, intrapersonal, or naturalist.

Verbal/Linguistic: The ability to think and communicate in words and text.

Authors, poets, journalists, speakers and educators often exhibit high degrees of linguistic intelligence. In musical terms, this intelligence may manifest itself as the ability to recall or create lyrics to songs or to learn lyrics quickly. Verbal aspects of music extend beyond the learned syntax of a given language. Through verbal explorations, we can imitate the sounds of musical instruments, thereby learning the language of the drum. Indian musical traditions teach using *bols*, syllabic representations of drum sounds used to vocalize the rhythms of the tabla and other drums. Many cultures use vocal sounds interchangeably with drums and percussion. The popular phrase "If you can say it, you can play it" is echoed by teachers and students around the world as more and more learn to "speak" through their instruments and create music with their voices. Creating vocal percussion grooves in a circle reinforces the fact that *we are the drums* and the music really is inside us, not on the page or in the instrument. Verbal/linguistic comments often include information that is based on an understanding through words. For example, someone who relates to verbal information might say, "When I heard you saying 4–3–2–1, I figured you meant to stop since that is like a countdown to zero."

Mathematical/Logical: The ability to calculate, quantify and consider hypotheses based on information, numbers and scientific laws of nature. Scientists, accountants, engineers and programmers must possess this intelligence. In musical terms, it may present itself through an ability to conceive of musical form and arrangement, or as an advanced understanding of harmonic and rhythmic relationships. For example, learning an arrangement requires keeping track of beats, measures and phrases and may include complex rhythmic breaks and cues. Music can be arranged in complex forms that require as much focus and attention to detail in order to be understood as many geometric or algebraic equations. The complex rhythms of the Indian tabla player are not unlike the continually unfolding shapes and lines of fractal images, while the sequences and layers in a symphonic arrangement are akin to an architect's blueprint. Logical/mathematical statements often include quantitative or cause-and-effect information: "We traded 4-bar phrases four times each, then 2-bar phrases eight times each. Each series was the same length."

Visual/Spatial: The ability to think in three dimensions and perceive external and internal imagery; also, to create, transform and identify images and objects and to navigate pathways through space.

Pilots, sailors, painters, sculptors and architects often have highly developed visual/spatial awareness and thinking. Musically speaking, this intelligence may present itself as the ability to choreograph movements (such

Children use Boomwhackers® Percussion Tubes to create sculptures.

Kinesthetic/Bodily: The ability to use and manipulate objects, often with a great degree of physical skill, and to gain understanding through touch and movement.

Athletes, dancers, surgeons and crafts people all have a highly developed kinesthetic intelligence. In music, this intelligence may surface as a natural technical ability on an instrument, or the ability to learn to play with little or no instruction. Drumming is a very physical art form. From the raising of hands and arms to the rhythmic swaying of the body, drumming offers a full body experience in making music. Members of the Japanese Taiko group Kodo spend many hours each day conditioning their bodies in an effort to transcend the physical limits of the body and play their drums in a fluid and free manner. When performed with proper guidance, the physical aspects of drumming can have similar effects to those generated by an aerobic workout or practicing Yoga. When we play drums together, we not only feel our own bodies moving in rhythm with our instrument, we feel the waves of sound that are being generated by everyone else in the circle. The energy that is being put into the drums comes back to us in the form of sound waves, running through us and back into our instruments. As we feel the pulse of the group, we create and add to it at the same time. This is palpable musical synergy. Kinesthetic comments revolve around the body experience and movement: "Stepping to the beat really helped me feel the pulse. It's like I was 'playing' the floor."

Musical/Rhythmic: The ability to sense and identify differences and changes in pitch, timbre, tempo and rhythm. To feel and communicate ideas and emotions through sound and music.

Composers, musicians, poets, sound therapists and instrument builders must all apply this intelligence to their craft. This intelligence is not contingent upon life experience or language, and as a result, is capable of being developed from a very early age. Musically, this ability is often evident in people who exhibit perfect pitch; those who make vocal "sound effects" when they describe something; remember melodies; identify people, animals or instruments based on their sound; recognize rhythms and melodies in words and phrases; and have the ability to hear music in everyday sounds. Poets work with the musical nature of words. To the poet, the sound quality of the word is just as important as its meaning. Musical statements often refer to something's rhythmic or tonal qualities: "German is staccato—while French is more legato." (The statement itself may even be musical!)

Interpersonal: The ability to interact with and effectively communicate with others.

These people are often good listeners and are able to "read" people so as to gain insight into their thoughts and emotions. Teachers, social workers, therapists and actors are often people who relate well to others. An example of this intelligence may be reflected musically in a heightened sensitivity to the emotional qualities or 'message' of a piece of music or the ability to communicate meaning

Students communicate through Boomwhackers® percussion tubes.

through music. When we are in a circle playing usic together we are a living, breathing entity, a community where each one of us has a part to play and where each of us is needed. We are working together to create a "community song" that changes moment-by-moment. We must be present and constantly interacting with the other participants—looking, hearing, seeing, moving and being together. Interpersonal statements generally refer to other people and note qualities of emotion or attitude: "I could sense a greater connection between the participants once we started playing together. It's as if music was our first language."

Intrapersonal: The ability to gain an accurate perception of oneself and use this information as a guiding factor in one's life.

This kind of "reflective thinking" is evident in philosophers, theologians, psychologists and spiritual guides. This intelligence could be expressed in musical terms in an increased capacity to draw analogies between musical and personal relationships (such as the steady pulse of a drum and one's own determination). Playing a drum or percussion instrument allows us to look at our own body language. How we are is how we drum—there's no hiding. Examining our own comfort levels with regards to self-expression can help us gain insights into where we feel confident or reserved, pushed or pulled and closed or open. Taking the initiative and trying something new through music can open up a side of ourselves that has been dormant, and build a greater sense of self-worth in other areas of our lives as well. Intrapersonal statements are often centered around how one feels about an experience or noting a change in perception or perspective: "When I started playing my drum in the group, I felt like I could express my true feelings, without the added anxiety of performing."

Naturalist: The ability to observe objects and events in nature and understand natural systems and patterns.

This intelligence is evident in hunters, farmers, ecologists and meteorologists. Musically speaking, this intelligence could manifest itself through one's ability to draw parallels between natural rhythms and cycles and those found in musical works. Some composers have modeled their works after "natural" events. The programmatic music of Vivaldi's *Four Seasons* and Gustav Holst's *The Planets* are two examples. The Paiste cymbal and gong company has produced a series of nature-inspired gongs that resonate to frequencies that relate to the nine planets in our solar system. Naturalist statements may include information linking music to organic events or objects: "When we play music together, it's like we're all traveling down the same river which helps us feel more connected to each other, all part of the same flowing rhythm."

LIVING IN RHYTHM

We are living in rhythm when we are walking our true path

We are living in rhythm when we are singing our true song

We are living in rhythm when we are dancing our true dance

We are living in rhythm when we are embracing our true self

—Kalani

Chapter 8

 **Music Games**

The following games and activities are fun, engaging, cooperative learning opportunities for students of all ages. As only you, the facilitator, know how to best serve the needs of your group, I leave it to you to decide which games are suitable for what age groups and how to modify them for special populations. For example, a music therapist may choose to simplify an activity for a group of developmentally disabled adults, while an elementary school teacher may make the same activity more challenging for a group of advanced students. Movements may be scaled down for a group of elderly participants, while a recreational activity director may add to the physical element in an after-school program for teens.

Although I use the term "students" in all of the descriptions, the term "participants" could just as easily be applied. I have presented these activities with children as well as adults. They can be used in your programs whether the overall goal is education, team building, therapy or just plain fun. I encourage you to experiment with these games and expand on the process and elements of each one, presenting them in your own way and in your own style. These are only starting points from which to launch your group's imagination. Explore them and see where they grow!

The following features are specified for each game and activity: title, time span, instruments, other materials (if needed), focus, the applicable National Standards for Music Education (**NS**),[2] multiple intelligences addressed (**MI**),[3] music therapy applications (**MT**), preparation, process, extension, and discussion.

For more Drum Circle Music games like these, see *The Amazing Jamnasium*.

Rumble Ball

A real crowd-pleaser! This game works for all ages and involves the entire group in a way that makes it easy for everyone to participate. Students work with basic musical concepts such as timbre and volume, and associate musical ideas with movement. Good for visual learners. Drumming has never been so playful!

Time span: 5–10 minutes

Instruments: hand percussion, drums

Suggestions: Use members from all four timbre groups (drums, wood, shakers, metal).

Other materials: a small rubber ball

Focus: improvisation, matching sound with movement, performing on instruments, active participation, leadership, spatial awareness

NS: 2 (performing), 3 (improvising), 4 (composing), 5 (reading), 7 (evaluating)

MI: visual/spatial, musical/rhythmic, kinesthetic/bodily

MT: creativity, group teamwork, leadership skills, motor skills (playing and using the ball), social interactions, taking turns, attention span, and self-esteem

Preparation: Form a large circle. Provide students with a variety of drums and percussion instruments.

Process

1. Upon entering the circle, play with the ball for a couple of minutes without giving instructions to the students. Establish three modes of play: bouncing, rolling, and tossing.

2. Ask students to provide adjectives that best describe the action of the ball bouncing on the floor. Example: sudden, hard, low, etc. **Tip:** When working with children, ask for a volunteer to define the word "adjective" for the group.

3. Ask students which instruments or instrument groups are best described by the adjectives they provided.

   Example: The drums and wood instruments sound hard and low, therefore, they work well as the bouncing sounds.

4. Invite students with the appropriate instruments to play along with the specific action. "Let's hear everyone with drums and wood sounds play when the ball bounces on the floor." Take a minute to practice with that group.

5. Repeat steps 2–4 for the actions rolling (sustained sounds—shakers, etc.) and tossing (high sounds—bells, tambourines, etc.).

6. Play with the ball using all three modes, and have students match the movements.

7. Add another student to share the ball with you, and then substitute another student for yourself. Change leaders often to give everyone an opportunity to lead (the new leader swaps instruments with the previous leader).

Extension

- Ask students if they can think of other actions to link up with the sounds, such as holding still, spinning on the floor, balancing it on one's head, etc.

- Substitute body percussion or vocals for instruments.

- Use balls of different colors to cue different arcs (sections of the circle) or instrument groups.
- Use Orff instruments grouped by pitch or instrument type.
- Use an "invisible" ball.

Discussion

- What did you like about this activity?
- Did you see a leader create a new action? How did you respond?
- What are some other actions we could match with sound?
- Do we need a ball to do this activity?

Let's All Play Our Drum!

This game always keeps students on the edge of their seats, listening carefully, and ready to PLAY! It's perfect as an interlude to an ongoing jam session or as an elimination game. Students benefit greatly from taking the leader position where they will be challenged to make full use of their rhythmic skills.

Time span: 10–15 minutes

Instruments: drums, percussion and/or body percussion

Suggestions: Provide a variety of instruments from all four timbre groups (drums, wood, shakers, metal).

Focus: active listening, responding to cues, rhythm and tempo awareness

NS: 2 (performing), 3 (improvising), 4 (composing), 6 (listening), 7 (evaluating)

MI: verbal/linguistic, musical/rhythmic, mathematical/logical

MT: creativity, leadership, self-esteem, short term memory development, sequencing, modeling behaviors, communication, social interaction, reality orientation, sound discrimination, attention span, impulse control, taking turns, motor skills

Preparation: Have everyone form a circle (standing or sitting). Provide an assortment of drums and percussion instruments.

Process

1. Ask everyone to stand, leaving the instruments for the moment.
2. Have the group match your actions for the capitalized words (one note only) as you introduce and combine the following cues:

    "Let's all clap our HANDS"

    "Let's all snap our FINGERS"

    "Let's all pat our THIGHS"

    "Let's all stomp our FEET"

    Note: Use the rhythm Ti–Ti–Ti–Ti–Toe for the above examples. Present one example several times through before adding the next.

3. Ask students to suggest other actions:

    "Let's all ? our ? "

    Add the students' ideas to the first four and continue, changing the tempo and subject of the cues.

4. Orbit the leadership role around the circle, inviting students to provide new actions.

5. Move to the instruments and present phrases that cue specific groups of instruments:

"Let's all ring our BELLS"

"Let's all clack our BLOCKS"

"Let's all shake our RATTLES"

"Let's all play our DRUMS"

6. Continue the game with the new cues, pausing occasionally to ask the participants if they can suggest other possible combinations.

Extension

Variation 1

1. Let everyone know that when you say, "Let's all Play our Drum," that everyone is to play their instrument on "DRUM!" (one hit) no matter which kind of instrument they have.

2. Say the cue phrase at different tempos and volumes.

3. Shorten the verbal cue to "All Play our Drum!" and "Play our Drum!"

4. Transfer the cue to an instrument by playing the phrase as you say it, then only playing it. Continue playing the game, while varying the tempo and dynamics of the cue.

Variation 2

1. Introduce a longer phrase and play only on the last note (the word "fun" in the following example).

1	+	2	+	3	+	4	+	1	+	2	+	3	+	4	+
Let's	all	play	our	drum	be	-cause	it's	so		much		FUN.			

2. Take away some of the last words (notes) so participants have to feel the beat through a rest before they play. This becomes more challenging as the cue becomes shorter.

3. Ask everyone to try this with their eyes closed.

4. Vary the tempo to make this more challenging.

Discussion

- Did anyone suggest an action that you particularly liked?
- What made the cues easy or difficult to follow?
- What advice would you give to someone who was about to try this?
- What are some other phrases we could use as a cue?

Signals: Hands

Students create their own team-based notation in this fast-moving activity. This "get out of your seat and move to the beat" game involves creativity, social skills, visual cues and timing. It's also a great way to develop leadership skills, non-verbal communication, gross motor skills and teamwork—and the leaders get an arm workout!

Time span: 10–15 minutes

Instruments: drums & percussion, or body percussion

Suggestions: Try this with a variety or all the same type of instruments. For faster tempos, use instruments that can be played with both hands such as hand drums or temple blocks with two mallets.

Focus: associating sound with movement, creating and notating music, following non-verbal cues, teamwork, math concepts, spatial awareness, awareness of self and others

NS: 2 (performing), 3 (improvising), 4 (composing), 5 (notating), 6 (listening), 7 (evaluating)

MI: visual/spatial, musical/rhythmic, mathematical/logical, kinesthetic/bodily, interpersonal

MT: motor-skill development, leadership skills, self esteem, social interactions, attention span, reality orientation

Preparation: Form a large circle. Provide instruments.

Process

1. Step in rhythm and have students simply feel the beat without playing (pat your chest to show "feeling" the beat).

2. While continuing to step in rhythm, hold up one hand to signal playing one-note-per-beat (1/4 note) and invite students to play their instruments or clap along (accent the beat with your hand).

3. Hold up two hands to signal two-notes-per-beat (1/8th notes).

4. Lower hands to signal resting (still feeling the pulse).

5. Experiment with these three modes of play (1–2 minutes) then ask for a volunteer(s) to lead the group.

6. Add another student to follow the leader to create a 2-beat phrase (the leader is beat 1 and the follower is beat 2).

    Tip: Ask the leaders to make hand gestures to accent the notes of their beat as the group plays along. You may wish to pause and have a brief discussion with the group as to what would make it easier to follow the leaders.

    Examples:

    •Leaders will hold their position for at least four cycles to give the group a chance to adjust to the new rhythm.

    •Leaders will make clear movements, only changing after the beat and not on it.

    Music Therapy Note: This might prove to be a challenging activity for therapeutic applications. For best results, try a simplified version or only attempt this with high-functioning groups. The next game, Signals: Feet, may be a better choice as it provides a visual framework upon which to build.

one note   two notes   rest

Extension

- Have half the circle follow one person or group, and the other half follow another person or group.

- Add more leaders to create even longer rhythmic phrases (3, 4, 6, or 8 beats).

- Design different signals for rhythms and dynamics (shaking hands for a roll, hand shapes to indicate techniques such as scraping, fingers only, staccato (short sounds), legato (long sounds)

- Transfer the rhythm(s) of the group to standard or iconic notation.

- Designate the leader's right hand as the downbeat and the left as the upbeats.

- If changing signals on-the-fly is difficult, try having the leaders form a new pattern during a 4-beat break (rest), then have the group play the new pattern four times through. Start a new pattern with the 4-beat break each time to allow the leaders time to change their signals.

1–2–3–4	1–2–3–4	1–2–3–4	1–2–3–4
Play	Play	Play	Change

Discussion

- What was challenging about this activity?

- What advice would you give to someone who was about to try this?

- Is there another name for what the leaders were providing? (Hint: Notation)

- What are some other ways music can be "notated"? (Hint: artwork, clothing, structures, etc.)

- What would make it easier to do the next time?

- Can you think of some other ways the leaders could signal musical elements?

Pieces of Eight

This is a wonderful game that shows students the principle of synergy—when the result is greater than the sum of their individual effects. It's also a great way to illustrate the beauty of simplicity, diversity and working together to create music that is unique and always "in the moment."

Time span: 10–15 minutes

Instruments: drums and percussion

Suggestions: A variety of hand drums, wood sounds, shakers and metal; Boomwhackers® percussion tubes or separate Joia tubes.

Focus: Active participation, concentration, composing and arranging music, teamwork, listening, diversity appreciation, math concepts

NS: 2 (performing), 3 (improvising), 4 (composing), 6 (listening), 7 (evaluating)

MI: logical/mathematical, rhythmic/musical, interpersonal

MT: cognitive skills, sequencing, reality orientation, motor skills, impulse control, self-esteem, taking turns, following directions, attention span

Preparation: Gather students in a circle. Distribute instruments.

Process

1. Ask students to silently choose a number from 1 to 8. Explain that you will be counting out loud from 1 to 8 in rhythm (repeating).

2. Ask students to play one note on their instrument each time you reach their number.

3. Clap in rhythm and count for the group. (You can stop counting out loud once the students are playing on their own.) Invite everyone to listen to the drum melody that results.

4. Suggest they try to find the people who are playing on the same beat as they are.

5. After a couple of minutes, suggest that everyone adds one note (playing 2 notes per each 8-beat phrase).

6. If desired, add more notes over time.

7. When it feels appropriate, reduce the number of notes by one until everyone is back to playing 1 note per 8 beats.

8. Bring the activity to a close by saying "Last time through," or cue a fade out.

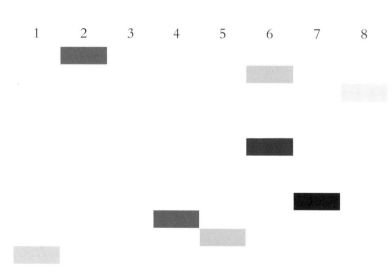

The music is full, even when everyone only plays one note!

Extension

- Group the circle into arcs, featuring one arc at a time while the others rest and listen. Rotate through the arcs in even phrases (four or eight phrases of 8 beats, for example). Reduce the number of phrases so the playing orbits more quickly around the circle.

- Create two phrases of 8 and have participants play on different numbers in each 8-beat phrase or play only one note for both phrases (1 note per 16 beats).

- Increase or decrease the tempo and/or volume.

- Have everyone play on the beats of their birthday. Example: 25th plays on 2 and 5, 14th plays on 1 and 4, 6th plays on 6, 29th plays on 2 and ?

- If playing hand-held percussion, have them move and form groups whose members are playing the same beats. Have them choose a different beat and form new groups.

- Have everyone play a different sound when a certain cue is given, such as brushing the head of a drum with the fingers, tapping the edge, or playing the person's instrument to your right.

- Try this as a movement exercise where all the members take a step (or play a body percussion sound) on their number(s).

Discussion

- What was challenging about this activity?

- Was there something you did that made it easier?

- Did you notice anyone doing something that you especially liked?

- Did everyone need to play a lot of notes for the music to sound full?

- Did the music remind you of anything?

- What would this look like in a drawing?

Chapter 9

Specific Populations

The drum circle format lends itself to many applications, from educational games for children to team-building activities for corporations and therapy for people with disabilities. As a Drum Circle Music facilitator, you may specialize in one or more of these areas, creating specific programs that address the unique goals of the population you are serving. This chapter focuses ways to address four specific population categories:

COMMUNITY

EDUCATIONAL

TRAINING & DEVELOPMENT

HEALTH & WELLNESS

Each population has its own "culture," whether it's education, health & wellness, training or community functions. Each has its own vocabulary of terms that identify how its members think and what is important to them. For example, an educator might make a request like, "We would like to provide our students with an inclusive environment that promotes creative thinking," whereas a corporate client might state, "We are looking to increase efficiency by improving our communication skills." By learning the language of each group you work with, you help them feel better about choosing you as their facilitator and also improve your ability to design programs that meet their needs.

Effectively addressing the goals of a specific population often requires knowledge and strategies that extend beyond the basics of drum circle facilitation. Keeping in mind that a drum circle is the vehicle to help us transport a group from one place to another, we must still learn how to successfully navigate the unique terrain where our journey will unfold.

Community Circles for the General Public

Community drum circles take place in a wide variety of settings, from gatherings in parks and beaches to jams in music stores or retreat & community centers. They are often open to the public and host a variety of people, from beginners to advanced players, and from children to the elderly. People come to community circles for a variety of reasons ranging from simply wanting to make music to the desire to forge deep spiritual connections.

The various kinds of community circles include the following:

Public circles
Celebration circles
Music store circles
Ceremonial circles

Public Circles

Drum circles are happening all the time. Many of them are non-facilitated free-form jams such as the Venice Beach, California drum circle (VeniceBeachDrumCircle.com). Community drum circles are the "ancestors" of all others. They are the original version, open to anyone who wishes to join the circle and play along. While these circles are generally non-facilitated, many of them do have regular hosts or an acting contact person or organizer who helps with logistical issues and offers assistance when people need it—staying out of the way the rest of the time. Public circles have regular schedules and loose time frames. People come and go throughout the event. Rhythms start, last for a while, then stop or change when the time is right.

Special thanks to Michael J. Marcionetti, MT-BC, for his contributions to the content regarding music therapy in the section "Health & Wellness Circles for Therapy or Fitness."

Michael J. Marcionetti, MT-BC, is a board-certified music therapist at the Austin, Texas, State Hospital, and a TOCA Percussion facilitator. He works on designing and implementing new studies that examine the effects of facilitated group drumming on symptoms of psychiatric patients.

Ways you can support a public drum circle:

- Introduce yourself to the host (if you're not the host) and let them know that you're there to help out.

- Play a steady pulse on a bell or bass drum. Be the foundation for your community.

- Help "newbies" find and play an instrument that is right for them.

- Facilitate change only when asked or needed.

Note: By nature, community circles include all kinds of people with a wide variety of personalities and lifestyles. Before bringing a child to any public circle, it's a good idea to visit it by yourself first to determine if it is suitable for you or your family.

> *If someone said, "Write a sentence about your life," I'd write, "I want to go outside and play."*
>
> **—Jenna Elfman**

Celebration Circles

Many community groups hold drum circles as a way of bringing people together to celebrate a special event. These circles are often well organized, start and finish at set times and may be facilitated. In this case, the facilitator supports the community by using a light touch, stepping in when needed and allowing for spontaneity. The main difference between a celebration and a public circle is intention. In a public jam, people are there for their own reasons; in a celebration, they are often there for the same reason. In this setting, the facilitator may also act as emcee, making announcements, introducing key people and leading the group in a song or chant that reflects the reason they have come together.

Ways you can support a celebration circle:

- Learn about the event, its history, and the reason it is being held.

- Work with the organizers to plan and promote the event.

- Facilitate the event using the DCM approach.

The Family That Plays Together...

I was on winter break from college, visiting my family during the holidays. We had just finished opening our gifts to each other when my mom appeared from the kitchen brandishing a wooden spoon and pot. "Show us some of that drumming you do when you're in school!" she called out as she "rang-a-tang-tanged" the pot. I quickly joined in by grabbing a couple of small kindling logs near the fireplace and started to play some of the larger logs that sat nearby. My brothers and step-father joined in on empty boxes, wrapping paper and whatever else was lying around, and the room was filled with a joyful noise in no time. We bipped and bopped, changed and tanged everything in the room for what seemed like the better part of an hour, trading "instruments" often and making up new rhythms and songs. Our recently opened gifts lay stroon about, forgotten in the musical activity and so obviously static among all smiles and laughs. Thanks to my mom's enthusiasm for music and fun, my family was experiencing its first drum circle. Now, more than 20 years later, it's a tradition around the holidays (and sometimes on just plain old days). Thanks, Mom!

Music Store Circles

Music stores are an obvious location for drum circles. They have the instruments, the space, and the staff to provide people with access to music-making activities in a friendly environment. The facilitator's role in a music store circle is to help the participants feel comfortable when playing drums and percussion instruments, and to provide some basic technical instruction and musical guidance for the group. People come to music stores because they want to learn how to create their own music and have fun doing it. Sometimes they feel intimidated by the technical aspects of the instruments or insecure about their musical abilities and don't know how to get started. A drum circle provides them with a positive group music-making experience that is sure to encourage them to continue exploring their musicality. As facilitators, our main goal here is to encourage the participants to play and to help them have fun. Remember: It's not a music lesson. It's playtime.

Ways you can support a music store circle:

- Work with the store to plan and promote the event.

- Expose people to a wide variety of instruments.

- Encourage people to purchase from the store.

Social benefits for participants of music store circles:

- Ability to take part in a group activity where they can share ideas and techniques.

- Being part of a community network of information and support.

- Having a safe and non-judgmental environment for creative expression.

- Freedom to have a positive musical experience.

Benefits to the music store:

- Provides new market opportunities

- Reaches a diverse range of customers

- Creates more music makers

- Boosts hand percussion sales

- Ongoing circles keep customers coming back

- Potentially provides new students for existing lesson programs

Ceremonial Circles

Many gatherings include drum circles as part of a greater ceremonial structure. Group drumming has long played a historic role in numerous world cultures, many of which have specific rites and practices. Always take care to show respect for the traditions of a particular people. We should avoid copying or replicating customs that we don't fully understand or are not part of our inherent culture. We may, however, create our own rituals and traditions that reflect in many ways the same structure, intentions and values of other cultures. The following will help you present an event that follows a simple ceremonial format.

Purification (Clearing the Space)

The area within which a ceremony is to take place may be *cleared,* or purified, beforehand. Clearing can take many forms, but the intent essentially remains the same: to purify the circle, release negative energy, and make room for inspiration. Purification can involve *smudging,* which is the burning of incense, tree sap, grasses or sage, or can be accomplished by sonically clearing the space with instruments such as finger cymbals, small bells, or chimes. In some Native American traditions, the area is smudged in the Six Directions: North, East, South,

West, Above and Below. Individuals may choose to be smudged as well.

In addition to first clearing the space with smudging and sound, I sometimes offer a personal "clearing" that involves washing the hands with salt-scrub. This gesture is symbolic of "washing away any limiting beliefs, and entering the circle with a clear mind and heart." It also feels great! How you choose to clear the space is up to you and your partners, but the purpose is universal.

> **Tip:** Ask people if they are sensitive to smoke or perfumes before you begin and modify your plans accordingly (perform sonic smudging or some other method as a substitute, for example).
>
> Ask people if they would like to be smudged individually before performing individual clearing.
>
> Always make it known to everyone in the group that it's OK not to take part in any aspect of a ritual or ceremony they do not feel comfortable with. It is not the action that is most important, but the intention behind it. Allow everyone the freedom to do what feels right for them.

Orientation (Inclusion)

In the orientation step, we seek to define the circle as it shall be for the duration of the event. The space has been cleared and now it is defined, not only physically, but metaphysically. The physical lines of the circle take shape as well as the lines of presence. The participants are engaged and focused. They are tuning in to the purpose of the event and are ready to begin. The circle is created and held by the participants through mutual agreement. At this point we acknowledge that we have come together in community for a common purpose. The circle is set and will remain intact until it is closed. Orientation to the circle may be acknowledged through simple acts such as forming the physical circle. It may be strengthened through interpersonal activities such as community greetings, declarations of purpose and through inclusion activities, such as playing or moving together.

Offering (Deepening Inclusion)

Once the circle is cleared and orientation has taken place, the participants may offer a devotion that is manifest in either a simple statement of gratitude or a material offering. A statement of gratitude may simply be an acknowledgement that the occasion is a unique gift shared between people, all of whom are important and needed for the event to be all it can be. It can also be a

message that conveys a feeling of thanks and of giving. Physical gifts may be placed in a centerpiece or type of altar. They can represent some aspect or purpose of the event (such as a special photograph or symbol) or they can be simple, everyday objects (such as a set of keys or a comb) that signify the importance of all things, large and small, and acknowledge that "everything in our lives is sacred." If a physical centerpiece might interfere with other aspects of the circle such as movement, verbal offerings and affirmations may take their place. Even the gesture of lighting a candle or a simple moment of silence can bring about a feeling of gratitude and set the tone of inclusion and presence within the group.

Dedication (Cooperation)

Once the offering has been made, the circle is completely open and activities may commence. These can take many forms including drumming, singing or *toning* (singing a single word or sound), meditation, and moving together. Themes of dedication include mutual support, working towards a common vision, shared responsibility, and commitment to achieving the best possible outcome. A facilitator's involvement at this stage will depend on the goals and needs of the group.

Integration (Appreciation)

To bring the ceremony to a close and gain the maximum benefit from the time spent in dedication, the participants may share statements of praise and knowledge. This is a time to publicly recognize one another's gifts and contributions, to draw analogies between activities that took place and other life experiences to deepen the meaning and internalize the knowledge, and to acknowledge the shift into a new state of awareness. Closing prayers, good wishes, and blessings may be offered at this time as well as songs and time for quiet meditation.

Educational Circles for Children

Perhaps the one group that appreciates participating in a drum circle most are children. All children love to make noise, move, have fun and use their imaginations to explore their creativity. Working with children as an educator, therapist or recreational activity director can be very rewarding, and participating in drum circles can help children learn about many aspects of music while providing a fun and dynamic environment for creative exploration. Children give immediate feedback and are honest and open to trying new things. The energy and spirit that comes from a group of children is free-flowing and, for the most part, unrestricted. But enthusiasm that is not channeled efficiently can create situations where facilitators may feel as if they are "losing the group." The following strategies and guidelines will help you to keep your groups focused and your activities flowing.

Learn to Stop Before You Start

Before you start playing instruments with a group of children, establish a way to stop together. This is like making sure your brakes work before riding your bike down a big hill! The following example works well:

1. Demonstrate a short, rhythmic phrase, such as "Shave and a hair cut—two bits."

2. Repeat the rhythm and ask everyone to listen carefully and shout "two bits!" along with you.

3. Play the rhythm on a cowbell and ask everyone to clap the "two bits" rhythm with you.

4. Practice this a few times with the group at different volumes and tempos.

5. Create other activities for the "two bits" cue such as freezing or holding up two hands.

During your program, you can use the "two bits" cue to bring the group to a stop.

Many classroom teachers will clap a simple rhythm that the group knows to echo back. It's a great way to get everyone's attention and have them focus on the facilitator. Another common tool used by many teachers is to create a special hand signal that means "Quiet—no playing or talking." The "peace sign" works well for this. Ask them to make the sign with you as soon as they see you make it. Make it into a contest! If you're working with a group that meets regularly, you might want to ask them if they have a "quiet sign" and use that one.

> *Never help a child with a task at which he feels he can succeed.*
>
> **—Maria Montessori**

Keep Things Moving

Children love movement and activity. When they don't have something to do, they create something to do. In order to avoid having a large group of children doing their own thing in the midst of a program (which isn't always a bad thing), it's best to decide how you're going to segue or link activities together before you start. If you're doing a movement activity, figure out where everyone will be when it's over and how they will get into the next activity. If you're ready to collect instruments, make a game out of it. Always give clear instructions before you start a group in motion, and include information that lets them know what to do when they're done with the current activity. For example, you might say, "When I start clapping, walk in rhythm as you put away your instrument, then sit and clap with me when you're done." I like to use non-verbal cues as much as possible when working with children because many of them may still be developing their verbal/linguistic skills. By having them match my movements, I can direct the flow from within the group. This allows us to do things together rather than placing me in an authoritative role, giving out commands such as "Everyone stop playing!" Instead, we simply do it together through matching.

HAIKU

No one listening
People playing many notes
Cacophony reigns

Do First, Talk Second

Children like to do things kinetically (in motion). Listening to someone talk about an activity does not hold as much appeal for young spirits as jumping in and experiencing it for themselves. If you feel that there needs to be time during your event for explanations about process or for talking about the history and techniques of an instrument, I recommend taking time after an activity to talk briefly with group. Sometimes the best way to start an event is by not talking at all. This can be captivating for children who are wondering what you're up to and may cause them to pay extra attention because they don't want to be left out! It has been my experience that talking loudly to a noisy group is the worst way to get their attention. Speak softly instead. When they realize they can't hear you, they will most likely bring down their own level. By raising your voice to be heard over the noise of a group, you imply that their current volume is acceptable because you are adapting to it. If talking softly works, you can use that experience to discuss the concepts of relative volume and contrast. It may be helpful to remind the children that their instruments "talk" when they're being played. When the children are listening, see if they can make their instruments "listen" as well.

HAIKU

A child's face lights up
They are making the music
They feel inside

Organize the Distribution of Instruments

Children will start playing an instrument as soon as it is in their hands. Passing out instruments while giving verbal instructions such as "Please don't play until everyone has an instrument" is like handing out glasses of milk to people who just ate a huge piece of chocolate cake and asking them to wait until everyone has milk before drinking theirs. If you are able to set up for your circle beforehand, place all the instruments under or in front of the chairs. Ask students to come in single-file and sit in the seat they reach as the seats get filled (or stand in front of a chair until everyone is in the circle). If you need to pass out instruments to a group that is already sitting, you could start passing them to one end of a row and ask students to pass them down until the row fills up.

Children have more need of models than of critics.
—Carolyn Coats

Another way to distribute instruments is by placing them in a single location such as a large box or a corner of the room where students can choose their instrument after being called on to do so. I often use random ways to decide which children get to choose their instruments first, for example, calling on everyone whose birthday falls in a specific month ("everyone born in March") or within a range of dates ("everyone whose birthday is between the 1st and the 10th of any month"). Fairness is a big issue with children. The more you can do to create a sense of equity, the less time you will spend settling debates about who "always" gets to play the triangle or who "never" gets to choose first. Rotate instruments often so that everyone gets a turn playing as many different kinds of instruments as possible. "Pass your instrument once to the right."

Playing Basics

Some general playing guidelines can help children achieve greater success and safety when using small hand percussion instruments.

Guidelines for playing instruments that are struck with sticks:

- Hold your instrument and stick(s) at waist-level.
- Keep a firm grip on your instrument and hold it steady.
- Gently play your instrument with a stick, mallet or beater.
- Move your stick only between waist-level and shoulder-level (below eye-level).
- Be aware of others who may be around you so no one gets played by accident!
- Never use your stick to point at or touch someone.

Tip: When passing out pairs of sticks, have students hold both sticks in one hand until you give further instructions. This reduces the amount of "chatter" that can come from random playing.

Guidelines for playing hand drums:

- Use your entire hand with fingers together, and move your arm from the elbow rather than just using the wrist.

- Let your hand bounce off the drumhead (like jumping on a trampoline).

- Stay relaxed. If you feel tired or your hands get sore, stop playing. Use an alternative stick or mallet, or switch to a different instrument.

 Use Humor

I was presenting a cup-passing game to a group of third-grade students. Some of them complained that their cups had cracks, which drew everyone's attention to the condition of the cups rather than playing the game. To help illustrate the unimportance of having a plastic cup with no cracks, I had all the students break their cups (which cracked us up too!) We then continued playing the "broken-cup-passing" game. This lightened the mood and helped students realize that what we think may be important has little to do with our goal or how well we can work together. The key to humor is resiliency –being able to go with the flow and not take yourself (or a cup) too seriously.

> *Humor is a spontaneous, wonderful bit of an outburst that just comes. It's unbridled, it's unplanned, it's full of surprises.*
>
> **—Erma Bombeck**

Make Tasks Fun

In general, it helps to turn tasks into games. "Let's see how fast we can all get quiet when I make the sign." Use your imagination (and theirs) to create fun of doing routine tasks, such as putting the instruments away: "Let's pretend that the instruments are animals and they are all walking back into their cave." Also, ask for helpers: "Who wants to be in charge of collecting the sticks?" Get them to be a part of your team and remember to always be a part of theirs.

 # Training & Development Circles for Corporate Groups

Companies and organizations often seek ways to foster a sense of team spirit, create appreciation for the diversity within their group, and lower the effects of stress on employees. Drum circles have proven to be a valuable tool for reaching these goals and provide an alternative to traditional "talk and chalk" presentations or physically demanding outdoor activities.

Benefits of a Drum Circle Music session when used in corporate training settings:

- Illustrates the importance of diversity

- Broadens listening and communication skills

- Develops a sense of camaraderie among co-workers

- Reduces the effects of work-related stress and anxiety

- Strengthens team-working skills

Benefits to corporate clients:

- Drum circles often hold the kinesthetic charge of outdoor activities, but are accessible to all people.

- Because drum circles are music based, they offer the mental challenges associated with composing and arranging musical elements, which have been shown to increase a person's capacity for logical thinking and problem solving.

- Because music is a non-verbal form of communication, it allows people to share ideas and concepts that transcend the boundaries of language and culture. Such a format would be ideal for a multi-national corporation that wishes to bring together the members of its international community in a unifying experience.

- Because music is a universal language, everyone can participate—including the deaf. Deaf people can often feel the pulse of the music within their bodies and appreciate the effects of group drumming as much as hearing people do.

- Drum circles can be presented on- or off-site, require minimal setup and space compared to many team-building activities, and integrate well with other types of programs.

The same values and dynamics that produce a successful musical experience also apply to the workplace. These include cooperation, active listening, resilience, building on each other's strengths, appreciation of diversity, peer support, and effective communication.

Creating Value

A training program must be designed with specific goals and outcomes in mind. In order to gain value from participating in an event, participants must draw parallels between their experiences in the circle and their lives in the work place. This is accomplished through the use of analogy. For example: "Playing music with others is like being on a project team because we all have to be communicating and working together." By asking key questions, the facilitator can help the participants process their experiences and

It's the things in common that make relationships enjoyable, but it's the little differences that make them interesting.
—Todd Ruthman

apply valuable lessons to their personal and professional relationships. Post-processing the information gained during the event is a necessary step that is key to any training program. In many cases, the group may spend as much or more time in post-activity discussions as they did in the activity.

Some key questions a facilitator might ask the group:

- What function did the different instruments have in the music?
- How do the instrument's roles relate to the roles in your workplace?
- Were there any musical parts that were more important than others?
- Did the simple parts help the more complex parts stay together?
- What were the unifying elements and how did they work?
- What helped or hurt the group's functionality?
- What were some of the challenges and how did the group solve them?
- What would you do differently the next time?

The facilitator's goal is to help participants draw their own analogies and learn from the experience, not to define it for them. Each member of a group will see, hear and feel the experience in a different way. In acknowledging these differences, the power of diversity can function to unify and strengthen the group, utilizing the unique talents and ideas of each participant. The process in which a diverse group of people works together to produce a result that is beyond any individual's sole capacity is known as *synergy*.

Designing a Training Program

Create a clear description.

Keep in mind that you may be communicating your program information to someone who knows nothing about what happens during drum circles or how they work. Use clear language that is physically descriptive and free from poetic license or elaborate metaphors.

Here is an example of a vague description: "A drum circle reaches people in places they seldom access through words, providing them with a deep and moving experience." While this comment may be true on some levels, it doesn't provide the reader with much information that is specific to drum circles and only raises more questions: What happens in the drum circle? How does it reach them? What places? Deep into where? What is it moving?

This example uses a clearer statement: "A drum circle is a group of people who, by playing drums and percussion instruments together, experience what it feels like to work together in rhythm, which promotes a sense of group synergy, cooperation and accomplishment."

Know how it works.

It's important to understand how your approach or method produces results. Be able to explain how your program does what you say it does. If you don't know how your program works, how will you be able to tell someone else? Here are some examples to consider:

> "[My fantastic program] creates a sense of community because each participant is contributing to the music in a different and equally important way. All members have the freedom to be themselves so they are at their best. They are seen and heard by everyone else in the group, and as a result, feel needed and valued."

> "[My incredible program] reduces anxiety by providing a friendly atmosphere where participants have the freedom to explore their creative sides without the fear of being judged. They often find themselves in humorous situations shared by the group, which creates a feeling of support and camaraderie."

Educate yourself about the topic(s) of your program. If it's about teambuilding, read books or take a teambuilding seminar. Be able to present a teambuilding exercise without using drums. Remember: the drumming is the vehicle—**you** are the tour guide.

Important questions:

- What reasons would you give a client who asks why they should hire you?
- What is unique about your program?
- How is your program similar to, or better than, those of your competition?

Know your client.

Get to know as much as you can about the groups you are serving. How can you find out what their needs are? Ask them! By asking questions and carefully listening to your client, you are better able to serve them because you gain more insights into their thinking. Find out what their goals are, then investigate various solutions and create a program that addresses their specific needs.

Create an outline.

In order to better organize your activities and show a potential client how your program produces the results you promise, create an outline that includes descriptions and a timeline.

Sample Outline	
Program Name	Drumming up Business
Specific Population (*Identify who your program serves*)	Business: Human Resources: Staff or management
Program Goal (*Describe what your program does*)	Teambuilding, boost moral
How It Works (*Describe how your program meets the goals of this population.*)	As team members work together within specifically designed music-based activities, they form stronger bonds while developing listening skills, group synergy and camaraderie.
Program Elements (*Describe the various components of your program and how long each one takes.*)	**Shaking Hands**—A movement activity that gets everyone involved, focused and relaxed. (5 minutes)
	Build the Beat—A pulse-based activity for the whole group that brings everyone together in rhythm. (10 minutes)
	Listen Line—A listening activity that demonstrates the importance of paying attention to those who are close to you, while staying tuned into the rhythm of the entire group. (15 minutes)
	Sound Factory—A movement-based rhythm game that demonstrates the importance of timing and teamwork. (20 minutes)
	Connections—A team-based activity that requires concentration, observation and focus. (15 minutes)
	Periodic Debriefing—Discussions about what was experienced. (25 minutes)
Other (*Add any additional information you think would be helpful.*)	Participants do not need any music training and all the instruments are provided. Our facilitators will help everyone use the instruments safely.
Duration (*Indicate how long your entire program will take.*)	90 minutes

You may wish to create several different programs that focus on various goals. You could also include a price quote with your outline.

Business tip: Set your prices and stick to them. If your client doesn't want to spend as much as you are charging, offer them a different, more economical program rather than lowering your price. How much should you charge? Research what others charge for providing similar services.

 # Health & Wellness Circles for Therapy or Fitness

For centuries, drumming has been recognized as an activity that can hold the keys to physical and mental well-being. Research shows that developing one's rhythm can even improve mental functioning.

Some of the health benefits of group drumming:

- Reduced anxiety
- Emotional release
- Community support
- Physical conditioning

- Spiritual growth
- Heightened creativity
- Personal empowerment

There are two general categories of health-oriented group drumming applications: music therapy, and health & fitness.

Music therapy applications are for special-needs populations who may benefit from the therapeutic qualities of a group drumming activity. These programs are often designed and facilitated by music therapists, social workers, and councilors in facilities for people with mental illnesses, learning disabilities and other psychiatric needs.

Health & fitness applications are for people who enjoy active music making and the benefits gained from participating in a health-oriented drumming program. These include programs designed with physical and mental benefits in mind, and are best suited for recreational facilities, schools, and health clubs.

Music Therapy

If you wish to facilitate a Drum Circle Music event in a setting with special needs groups, there are a number of factors to consider.

The clients you are working with may represent several different diagnoses.

It is not uncommon to work with a large group of highly symptomatic clients. One can observe clients responding to internal stimuli, exhibiting symptoms of mania, making sexually inappropriate comments or gestures, and displaying a variety of other symptomatic issues. There are basic behavior modification techniques that can be used **if** a problem comes up during your session, though it is best to have a mental health professional working with you during the activity. Some people to involve in the group could be music therapists, recreation therapists, social workers, psychologists, or other licensed counselors.

Generally speaking, clients in a psychiatric setting will be very open to the drum circle experience, but in some cases the group may not be 100 percent participatory.

Sometimes just being in the room is significant for one client's therapeutic process. Each person in the group is an individual, and each individual is experiencing something different. In these groups, subtle facilitation from your seat or the edge of the circle usually works best. Usually a simple rhythm that you can stick to will be all the musical material you need for success. This can serve as an anchor for the group and gives the participants lots of room to express themselves.

> *What we forget as children is that our parents are children, also. The child in them has not been satisfied or met, or loved, often.*
>
> **–Edna O'Brien**

In many cases, the idea of playing a drum in a room full of relative strangers can be an anxiety-producing situation.

It is important to let the group know that you appreciate them and their willingness to contribute to the music. Often the discussion at the end of the music will turn into a very supportive verbal praise session from peer to peer. This can be crucial in developing positive social skills and the ability to reach out to one another. It would be helpful at this point in the experience to have a trained professional assisting the discussion. From time to time, deep emotional issues do come up that you may not have the expertise to handle. It is crucial to recognize your role in the therapeutic process, as drum circles with this population can be very cathartic and healing, but they can also be damaging without the proper guidance.

Goals of a Therapeutic Drum Circle

Reality Orientation and Self-Awareness

A drum circle is a nice tool for reinforcing reality-based behavior because of the in-the-moment aspect of improvisation-based music. The facilitator can open a discussion about aspects of the music after the completion of a piece. Some sample questions may include the following:

- What instrument were you able to hear the best?
- What did you like about Bill's pattern?
- What would have made the piece more musical?
- Tell me why you chose a maraca to play?
- What instrument would you like to try in our next circle?

All these questions are concrete and in the "now" of the musical experience.

Self Expression and Creativity

A drum circle provides a safe, supportive environment where clients can express themselves non-verbally and receive peer reinforcement. The facilitator could start a circle by asking the clients to play whatever they would like to say to the group on the drum. The group mirrors the rhythm back, validating and reinforcing the client's contributions. Another way to facilitate self-expression is to feature players during a groove.

Cognitive/Sequencing

In the psychiatric setting, it is important to maintain cognitive functioning. One way to stimulate thinking and conversation is to use the instruments as a focal point for a discussion about the cultures from which they originate. This will often lead to discussions in the group about personal heritage, cultural pride, and distant or recent memories. A facilitator can empower the clients to build the music in the drum circle by asking them to make up their own rhythms. When the music ends, it is helpful to have a facilitated discussion about the quality of the experience. Talking about the importance of individual contributions, being able to remember the patterns, and being able to play a specific rhythm within the context of a multi-layered song helps to reinforce short-term memory recall and increases insight into the cognitive skills necessary to create a successful musical experience.

Impulse Control

Impulse control problems such as name-calling, acting out in the group, response to internal stimuli, boundary issues, and sexually inappropriate behavior are all issues that can come up in a therapeutic setting. A drum circle is a tool we can use to work on impulse control by focusing on teamwork and the importance of everyone's contributions. Facilitation tools such as controlling volume, tempo, and the density of the music are extremely important in maintaining a sense of teamwork. For example: "It was great when the volume came way down and Mary was the first to notice. She played the tambourine so quietly. It was perfect! She must really be tapped into the group rhythm today." In a discussion, the facilitator can acknowledge participation and the ability of the clients to be creative within the structure of the music. During this discussion, sometimes it is helpful to go around the circle and have each client tell someone else what part they liked and why.

Communication/Social Interaction

A drum circle can be used to build non-verbal communication skills such as eye contact and body language. A great activity with which to start a group is an egg shaker pass. This activity encourages the clients to break out of their "personal space" and interact physically with others. It's nice because there is some physicality to it, but the activity can be accomplished in a seated position and the participants don't have to actually "touch" one another. They just have to place an egg in their neighbor's hand.

The Egg Shaker Pass *

1. Start with everyone sitting in a circle.

2. Hand out an egg shaker to each participant.

3. Ask everyone to hold out their **left** hand (palm up), and then place the shaker in it.

4. Ask the group to follow your motions (move slowly).

5. With your **right** hand, pick up your shaker and place it in the **left** hand of the person to your **right**.

6. As you pass your shaker to the **right**, the shaker of the person to your **left** should be placed in your **left** hand.

7. Move slowly and wait for those who may need a little more time.★★

8. Keep passing shakers until everyone is in the groove. Say a chant together or just listen to the rhythm!

9. Gradually speed up and enjoy laughing with the group as people start dropping their eggs!

10. Congratulate the group on a job well done. (The goal was to have fun!)

★ Thanks to Barry Bernstein, MT-BC for sharing this activity.

★★People sitting across the circle from you may mirror your motions and pass their shakers to their left. This is common and gives everyone a reason to laugh. Let them know it's OK and allow them time to adjust.

Relaxation/Stress Management

There are many stressors related to having a mental illness. Developing skills to combat and cope with stressors is extremely important to a client's recovery. Sometimes, before a group session starts, clients are invited to participate in deep breathing and progressive muscle relaxation exercises, some of which may include guided imagery.

> **Tip:** Do not use guided imagery under **any** circumstances when working with clients with psychoses. This can be extremely dangerous and destructive to such a person.

Physical Involvement/Motor Skills

Drumming is a great way to increase gross and fine motor skills. If the group focus is gross motor skills, use instruments that require large movements such as the bass drum, maracas, tambourine, cowbell, and shékere. When the group focus is on fine motor skills, provide instruments that use more finger movements such as frame drums, bongos, doumbek, small shakers or kalimbas. From time to time in a music therapy drum circle, clients will be moved to dance. Great! Go with it. As long as the dancing is socially appropriate, it should be encouraged. In some sessions, the entire group may be dancing by the end of the activity! When the clients are physically involved in making music, an increase in social camaraderie is noticed immediately following the group work.

Coping Skills

A drum circle can be a healthy environment for the development of coping skills such as self-reliance, resourcefulness, flexibility and the ability to relax and assess situations. Clients are encouraged to make up their own rhythms and songs in the controlled music therapy groups. Some participants are drawn to quiet, personal percussion instruments such as frame drums and mbira, while others are more drawn to the large community style drums such as jembe and conga. In the group, it is important to facilitate client choice so that members are empowered to determine their own musical path.

A Drum Is Not a Pillow

Therapists may be tempted to encourage some clients to "drum out their anger" on an instrument. While this may provide relief on some level for the client, it may not be the best use of a musical instrument. I strongly encourage therapists who wish to engage clients in a physical-release activity to use an appropriate tool such as a pillow or rubber bat. Doing so ensures clients are not being taught to "beat up" an instrument. Instead of "beating the drum," try "drumming the beat" to encourage positive thinking and teach respect for the instruments others have worked to provide.

Accessibility Creates Inclusion

When working with groups whose members may have a disability or heightened sensitivity to certain elements, you can help facilitate everyone's comfort and communication by following these guidelines:

- Use large print for handouts.

- Group together participants who are wearing fragrances.

- Ensure a wheelchair-accessible layout (aisles are 3-feet wide, ramps are appropriate, etc.).

- Do not touch or move a wheelchair without the user's permission. Whenever possible, sit down to speak one-on-one with a person in a wheelchair.

- Avoid flames and candles; use flashlights, chimes, and flags instead.

- Speak directly to the person with the disability rather than to the interpreter or attendant.

- If you believe someone needs your help, first ask if you may be of assistance and then receive their instructions instead of assuming you know what needs to be done.

- Touch the arm of the person who is deaf to get their attention when you can't catch their eye.

- When speaking to a deaf person, make sure your face, especially your lips, are clearly visible. Speak more slowly and distinctly than usual.

- Before speaking to the person who is blind, say the person's name. Identify yourself before continuing.

- Do not smoke near people who must avoid it. Close doors that let in smoke from outside.

- Turn off cell phones, pagers and any other electronic devices that could be disruptive to the group.

- Use language of equality: "mute" instead of "dumb," and "disabled" instead of "handicapped."

- Use person-first language: "a child with autism" instead of "an autistic child."

Health & Fitness

The following are all holistic, music-based programs that I developed to integrate drumming with other proven health-promoting strategies. They illustrate how drumming can be used to serve a variety of populations and may provide you with direction and/or ideas you can use in your own practices.

Living in Rhythm

The Living in Rhythm program is an example of how group drumming can be incorporated into health-promoting activities for adults. It is designed to help participants develop their capacity for vision, wisdom, power and healing through music, movement and meditation practices. Participants use a variety of drums and percussion instruments to create various settings for play, socialization, self-reflection and creativity. Drumming approaches range from the simple "shamanic-style" to complex polyrhythmic ensemble playing. Other activities include individual, partner and group movement, in addition to meditations, storytelling and journaling.

The benefits of this program include providing an enhanced sense of play, rhythm and confidence; freedom from self-judgment and limiting beliefs; integration of program concepts into life experiences; and the development of stress-reducing tools and activities. Other program goals include living through integrity, intuition, insight and truth; honoring self through music, dance, storytelling and silence; exercising objectivity, release and passion; overcoming addictions and obstacles to love.

One participant commented, "Living in rhythm was a lovely journey of self-reflection, self-discovery and joyous play."

The Jamnasium

Now, more than ever, our children and schools are in need of healthy activities that bring the arts and education together to help young people develop positive life habits. The war on sugar, junk food, smoking and inactivity needs to be fought head-on in our schools, community centers, boys' & girls' clubs and recreation facilities.

The Jamnasium combines drumming with physical activities and health education for young people. Children use drums, percussion instruments and sports equipment in specially designed programs that foster creative play, cooperation, teamwork, physical conditioning and health awareness. During the Jamnasium, children run, jump, move together in rhythm and chant songs that have positive health messages. By integrating fun and creative music-based activities with health-promoting information, we empower our children with the tools they need to take responsibility for their health and wellness as they develop positive life habits that will carry them into their adult lives.

Rhythm Gym

Rhythm Gym programs combine movement activities and drumming in a creative environment that promotes teamwork, socializing, healthy lifestyles, and fun. The concept for Rhythm Gym began in 2002 when I was looking for a way to combine two of my favorite activities: making music and exercising. I called it "Tashiko Fitness Drumming" and offered classes at my local gym. Rhythm Gym activities are an extension of my fitness drumming classes and feature a unique combination of strategies that have been proven to increase timing, coordination, social skills, confidence, and promote a general sense of well-being. Research tells us that people who feel like they are part of a community, are able to express themselves, and feel supported by their peers show lower stress levels and live happier lives. Rhythm Gym activities include free and coordinated movement, body percussion, toning/singing, and the playing of drums and percussion instruments. Socializing takes place in circles, partnerships, and small groups. Sessions close with sharing and guided relaxation. Rhythm Gym programs are largely based on my work as an Orff-Schulwerk practitioner, Drum Circle Music facilitator, amateur Yogi, and gymnastics instructor. With music and fitness programs being cut from school curriculum and more people looking for meaningful ways to connect with others in their community in a healthy way, these programs are needed now more than ever. Rhythm Gym is a 501(c)3 non-profit organization. To learn more, visit rhythmgym.org.

> *Those who think they have not time for bodily exercise will sooner or later have to find time for illness.*
>
> **—Edward Stanley**

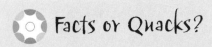
Facts or Quacks?

There is little doubt that group drumming can provide many health-related benefits and improve the quality of people's lives in many ways. Drumming is fun, creative, physical and social. It allows many people to share an experience together and to connect with one another on many different levels. When promoting the health benefits of drumming to our community or potential clients in any format, we must always take care to represent them in ways that are responsible and accurate. You may hear some people claim that drumming can realign your energy, change your cellular structure or thought patterns, specifically affect your immune system or have other predictable psychological or physical outcomes. Before you preach these benefits that are based on word alone, take time to research and learn as much as you can about the subject and about those making the statements. Find out if there are any other sources that support the claims. Was there a study done that shows evidence? If so, get a copy and read it. If it's too technical, see if there is a summary available. Seek the facts; consult quality medical resources; ask for clarification of claims until you understand the reasoning behind them. This way, you can develop strategies and programs that produce meaningful results, while preserving the integrity of your work.

Most of the health benefits of group drumming actually come from the social and emotional connections we gain from the activities rather than from the act of drumming. When we feel safe, valued, and able to express ourselves, we are happy and our stress levels drop. When stress levels fall, our bodies produce lower quantities of potentially damaging hormones, our blood pressure is reduced, "feel-good" hormones are released, and we become healthier as a result. It's that simple.

Healthy Sound Levels

It doesn't do much good to provide people with a health-oriented drumming activity that causes them hearing loss. As a facilitator, part of your role is to ensure that the total volume of your circle remains at healthy levels for your participants. What are healthy levels? According to studies by the World Health Organization (http://www.who.itl), sustained sound levels above 100 decibels (dB) can cause hearing damage. Even levels above 85 dB may cause hearing loss in as little as 1 hour. An indoor drum circle of 50 people can easily produce levels between 95 and 110 dB.

What can you do to help?

- Be aware of the volume levels and make adjustments to the music when needed.

- Children and the elderly may be especially sensitive to loud music. Use low-volume instruments when possible to reduce the overall sound levels.

- Present activities that feature part of the group while others listen, such as orbit or echo games.

- Balance loud points with quiet playing (fingers only) or create a sound scape through storytelling.

- Provide foam ear plugs for those who need them.

- Use the instrument guide on page to help you choose the appropriate instruments for your circles.

How Loud Is It?

Heavy city traffic: 85 dB

A standard blow dryer: 105 dB

A typical rock concert: 110 dB

Note: If you have to shout to be heard, the volume level is most likely over 100 dB.

And the Beat Goes On

Using the drum circle format to facilitate the goals of a specific population can be both challenging and rewarding. Music teachers, therapists and drum circle facilitators all over the world are discovering new ways to use group drumming to forge meaningful connections as they bring people together in rhythm. The best way to develop your particular style of the Drum Circle Music approach is to step into the circle, trust your intuition and be yourself. By creating your own programs and gaining experience, you become part of a worldwide community of music facilitators.

Remember:

- Whoever is in a particular circle is exactly who is supposed to be there.

- What happens is exactly what is supposed to happen.

- Every circle is a unique gift and learning opportunity.

- There is a community of people who support you and your work.

Final Thoughts

♥ Give from the Heart

"Come in baby. You hungry? Grandma's got some raw fish with limu that your cousin brought from the islands."

My grandmother's 4-foot-10-inch frame appeared in her doorway late one evening as she welcomed me into her home. "That's OK, Grandma. It's late. I can eat in the morning." (Grandma always wanted to feed her grandchildren.)

"Come sit down. Grandma's got some fresh poi and lomi salmon. Sit."

I sat at the kitchen counter where I always sat late at night in her house and watched as she pulled multiple dishes and bowls full of Hawaiian food from her refrigerator. This is Hawaiian style.

My Grandma always had Hawaiian food for her grandchildren. "Your cousins were here a couple of days ago, but I saved this for you!" She loved to see all her *kekis* (children) eat her food. I didn't mind, of course! I was enjoying my lau lau, lomi salmon, raw fish with limu and poi when she asked with a look of satisfaction, "You know why your Grandma's cooking tastes so good?"

"Why is that, Grandma?" Of course I knew the answer because we had the same conversation every time I sat there to eat, but I knew she liked telling me.

"It's because your Grandma puts love into the food."

I learned many things from my Grandma. One of them was how to make Hawaiian food with what the Hawaiian's call "aloha spirit," also known as putting love into what you do. She knew that her intentions came through in her cooking. "When your Grandma cooks, she uses her hands to make the food and prepare everything with care. Then when people eat it, they feel nurtured."

I, too, believe this is true—not just in cooking, but in everything we do.

You don't have to be Hawaiian to work with aloha spirit in your heart. Put love into what you do and those who experience it will feel it.

Mary Ann Kalama, 1904–1993

Much aloha to my Grandmother, and to all mothers who taught us to put love into our work.

I was presenting a Drum Circle Music session for about 300 music educators when I noticed an elderly woman who was beaming with joy. She was playing her drum with passion and had a big smile on her face. At one point, I asked if I might call upon her during the event. I wasn't sure why at the time—I just had an intuition. When it was time to close the circle, I thanked the sponsors and hosts (Peripole-Bergerault and TMEA) for providing us with the means to have such a great experience, then I called upon my new friend to come to the center of the circle. "Do you have a message for the other teachers, especially the new ones?" I asked. She gave a simple and beautiful message: *To teach with joy and passion and love your students and your work.* She was a perfect example of someone who was living in her rhythm, and showed that every circle of people is a resource for great wisdom. All you have to do is ask.

Remember the story at the beginning of this book about a girl who asked me why we have to learn music? At the end of my residency, she wrote me this note:

> Monica A. 11-10-03
> Kalani I like the bubbles and I had so much fun I learned a lot of music. The dance was fun I like your instruments. Some times I told my parents about it. I was even tired when we finished. I like music alot.
>
> I am still practicing music. I put some pails on the floor and prietent it was my drums and begin to play it. My parents clap at me when I do a good job. I am always proud of myself.

When you and your participants have traveled together through passages of time and looked across the circle at each other through rhythm-colored glasses, when the last thundering rumble gives way to the gentle *pa-pum pa-pum* of many hearts beating as one, when we have given ourselves a rhythmic hug that leaves our spirits glowing, we realize that all the activities, drumming, facilitation and games have simply been the vehicle that brought us to a place where differences are celebrated, creativity flows unrestricted, and spirits are renewed. Your participants may not remember the details of each activity you presented or any of the specific rhythms they played; they may not have learned much about how to read music or tune a set of bongos; but they will always remember one thing—the *feeling* they had when it was over.

A drum circle really *is* a people circle.

Aloha nui loa,
Best wishes to you on your journey.

Kalani

Appendix A

Instrument Guide

There are a wide variety of drums and percussion instruments available today. Many of them are well-suited for the drum circle and provide a multitude of options for participating in group music making. I recommend instruments made by Toca Percussion, Latin Percussion and Peripole-Bergerault, Inc., because of their high quality, durability, authentic sound and impeccable reputation. If you're not familiar with the instruments that comprise the "world percussion" family, take a few minutes to look over the following photos and descriptions. See and hear most of these instruments on the *Together in Rhythm* DVD.

Instrument Categories

Unpitched Percussion
Drums, Wood Sounds, Shakers & Scrapers, Metal Sounds

Pitched Percussion
Percussion Tubes, Barred Instruments and Plucked Instruments

Vocal & Body Percussion

UNPITCHED PERCUSSION

dundun

Harmony drums

 **Drums**

The DCMI symbol for drums is the circle, often associated with feminine energy, unity and healing.

Bass Drums

Bass drums have a low-pitched quality and are generally associated with foundation, pulse or heartbeat, and Mother or Earth.

Surdo

dundun (DOON-doon)   The West African bass drums are used in Malinke and Susu drumming and are played together with the jembe and other hand percussion.

Harmony drums   Developed by the Peripole-Bergerault company in association with Toca Percussion, these graduated floor drums provide younger students with tunable bass drums that are easy to play.

surdo (SOOR-doh)   This is a double-headed bass drum from Brazil, commonly used in samba bands to provide the underlying pulse for the music.

Stick Technique (for Bass Drums)

Larger sticks and mallets like those used for bass drums are best held at an angle to the forearm of 40 to 70 degrees, using all the fingers, and without the index finger placed on the back. To gain power and control without stressing the wrist, play bass drums by rotating the forearm (like turning a doorknob) rather than by bending the wrist.

Good Technique

Poor Technique

Note: Placing the index finger on top of any stick or mallet is not recommended. Doing so does not allow the stick or mallet to rebound off the drum, and the grip is generally less stable than when using all the fingers to hold the stick.

Hand Drums

ashiko (Ah-SHEE-koh)   A cone-shaped drum with African influences, featuring either rope or mechanical tuning. It sounds like a cross between the conga and the jembe.

ashiko

conga (KON-gah)   A single-headed, barrel-shaped drum that originated in Cuba, the conga is traditionally made of wood and produces warm, rich tones when played with the hands.

jembe (JEM-bay)   The jembe (or *djembe*, the traditional French spelling) is a West African drum that originated with the Malinke and Susu peoples located in modern-day Guinea and Mali. Its distinctive mortar shape and thin head produce a wide range of tones, from a deep bass sound to a high-pitched slap.

conga

Note: Encourage participants to position themselves in a way that allows for natural posture and arm movements. Instruct them to tip drums to the side or away from the body; tipping a drum towards the body may create wrist strain. Model proper techniques for beginners and suggest the removal of rings before playing hand drums. For more on hand drum techniques, I recommend Alfred Publishing's book & enhanced CD sets called All About Jembe *(20617),* All About Congas *(21453), and* All About Bongos *(21458).*

traditional jembe

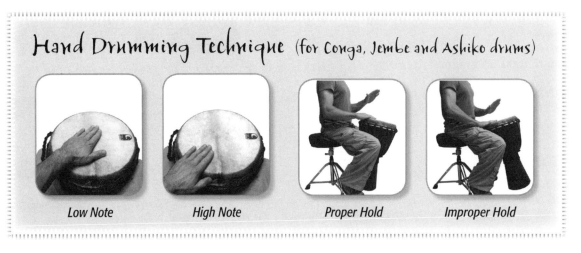

Hand Drumming Technique (for Conga, Jembe and Ashiko drums)

Low Note | High Note | Proper Hold | Improper Hold

modern jembe

bongos

bongo (bon-GOH)   The two small drums of a set of bongos are 6.75 inches wide and 8 inches wide in diameter, and are connected in the middle. They are often played with the hands, but sometimes sticks (such as the Vic Firth Rute 505) or mallets are also used.

doumbek (DOOM-bek)   This goblet-shaped drum was traditionally made of clay and fitted with a fish-skin head. Modern doumbeks are made of everything from aluminum to fiberglass and often feature plastic heads. They are placed in the player's lap and played with the fingers.

Sienta drums   This line of drums from Peripole-Bergerault features hand drums specifically designed for group drumming. Eliminating the need for players to tip the drums or use separate stands, the Sienta line features built-in stands that add stability and help the drums resonate by lifting them off the floor. The congas have legs while the jembes have openings at the bottom called *sound arches*. Stands are also available for Sienta bongos that hold the drums at a comfortable height while the player is seated (*sienta* means "sit" in Spanish).

doumbek

Sienta jembe

cajón (kah-HONE)   This wooden box drum is part of the musical heritage in certain regions of central South America (primarily Cuba and Peru). The player sits on the instrument and plays the thin plywood "head" with the hands, producing sounds that range from deep bass tones (center) to cutting slaps (top corners). The head is often loosened on the corners or backed with cords to produce a characteristic rattle or "buzz" when struck.

Sienta conga

cajon

Drum Technique
(for bongos and doumbek)

Low Note *High Note*

Note: Some of the drums we use in drum circles such as the doumbek, conga, bongos and jembe are traditional or classical instruments from other cultures. To show respect for the instruments and the cultures from which they come, I often include some background information for groups who may have never played these instruments before, and I encourage everyone to treat these instruments with the same respect and care they would give a violin, guitar or any other classical instrument. This means acknowledging that the drums are musical instruments, capable of being played at very high levels by professional musicians and not things to be used as tables or chairs. To discourage people from setting objects on the instruments, suggest that they be placed on their sides or covered when not in use. Of course, it's a good idea to extend this concept of respect to all the other types of percussion instruments as well.

Frame Drums

A frame drum (often called a *hand drum* in the music education field) may be defined as a drum that has one head and is wider than it is deep. It is perhaps the most common drum design throughout the world. Most frame drums produce a round, dark tone. In a drum circle setting, they are often played with mallets or sticks, but can also be played with the hands and/or fingers. Frame drums are preferred over flat "pancake-style" drums because they are durable, easy to hold, and sound great.

Some popular types of frame drums:

bendir (BEN-deer)   Middle Eastern

bodhran (boh-RAHN)   Irish

buffalo drum   Native American

tamborim (tam-boh-REEM)   Brazilian

tar   North African

Rainbow hand drums   This set of five graduated hand drums is available from Peripole-Bergerault, Inc. They are recommended for activities that would benefit from having drums of different colors.

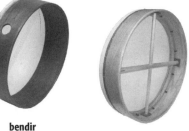

bendir

bohdran

buffalo drum

tamborim

tar

rainbow
hand drums

Wood Sounds

The DCMI symbol for wood sounds is the rectangle, the shape of wood blocks. In many cultures, sticks and bones are associated with ancestral knowledge, teaching and wisdom. Sticks and bones are thought of by many as the original or "first" percussion instruments.

clapper sticks   These long wooden sticks are cut down the middle and feature a hollow core that deepens the tone. They are found in Korean and Native American music.

clave (KLAH-vay)   Claves consist of a pair of hardwood sticks that are struck together. They are traditionally used in music from Latin America.

clapper sticks

claves

rhythm sticks Small pairs of solid wooden or synthetic sticks in various colors, sometimes featuring bumps that produce a rasp-like sound when rubbed together. Rhythm sticks are well-suited for children.

slit drum, or **tongue drum** This drum is made by cutting the top of a wooden box to form keys of various pitches. It is played with rubber mallets. *Note: Some slit drums, such as those made by Michael Theil (Hardwood Music) are tuned to specific pitches and scales.*

slit drum

tone blocks, or **temple blocks** These sets of graduated wooden blocks produce a hollow sound when struck with a stick or mallet.

tone blocks

two-tone blocks The two high and low woodblocks of this set are on a handle and played with a small wooden stick or mallet.

two-tone blocks

woodblock A small section is carved out of these solid blocks of wood, creating an instrument that produces high, clear tones when struck with a stick or mallet.

plastic two-tone blocks

woodblock

 Shakers & Scrapers

The DCMI symbol for shakers, rattles and scrapers is the star, associated with birth, purity and honor. The rattle is associated with the warrior archetype in some cultures, used as a cleansing tool. Rattles are often given to infants as comfort items. The sound has been said to resemble that of a mother's voice when heard from inside the womb, which has been recorded as a high-pitched buzzing sound.

axatse

axatse (ah-HAH-chee) This rattle is designed like a shékere and is about the size of a maraca.

cabasa (kah-BAH-sah), or **afuche** (ah-foo-SHAY) Metal chains are wrapped around a specially textured stainless steel cylinder with a handle. When rotated, the chains scrape against the cylinder to produce sound.

cabasa or afuche

caxixi (kah-SHEE-SHEE) These basket shakers are filled with small pebbles or beans and features a piece of gourd, plastic or metal at one end.

egg shaker Egg shakers come from the nests of the ever-elusive shaker bird. They come in a variety of colors and are great for passing games or for practicing your incubation techniques.

caxixi

egg shakers

frogs & crickets These were never so easy to take care of. All you have to do is stroke their backs or bellies with a wooden stick and they'll *sing* for you!

guira (WEE-rah) This metal cylinder is from the Dominican Republic and played with a multi-pronged metal scraper.

frog & cricket

guiro (WEE-roh) This Afro-Cuban scraper is made from a hollowed gourd and played with a small wooden stick.

maracas (mah-RAH-kahs) A maraca is a hollow bulb on a handle that is filled with small pellets such as beans or pebbles.

guiro

puili sticks (poo-EE-lee) Puili sticks are Hawaiian instruments made sections of bamboo that are cut lengthwise to produce many thin strips. When played, they are struck against each other and on the player's shoulders.

guira

maracas

Hawaiian puili sticks

rain stick   The rain stick is a pellet-filled tube fitted with many small cross-sticks, and produces a gentle rain-like sound as the pellets fall from one end of the tube to the other.

reco-reco (HEH-koh HEH-koh)   This Brazilian-style scraper is similar to the guiro and traditionally made from bamboo.

seed pod rattle   These clusters of small and large seed pods have been used for centuries in the music of Central America, South America, and many African countries.

shékere (SHAY-keh-reh)   The shékere is a hollowed gourd fitted with a veil of beads. It is commonly used in Caribbean and West African music.

tube shaker   A tube-shaped container made of metal, plastic or wood that is filled with small pellets such as beans, pebbles, rice or shot. Some shakers feature multiple cylinders that are joined together.

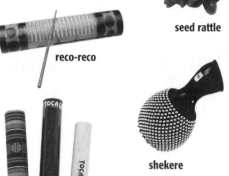

rain sticks

seed rattle

reco-reco

tube shakers

shekere

 Metal Sounds

The DCMI symbol for metal sounds is the triangle, often associated with male energy, stability and vision. In many cultures, bells are found in places of thought and reflection such as temples, churches and schools.

agogo (ah-goh-GOH)   Two cone-shaped bells are attached by a metal rod or spring and played with a small wooden stick (*timbale* stick).

cowbell   Cowbells come from cows that have had their bells taken away. They come in many shapes and sizes and are usually played with a stick or mallet.

finger cymbals   These two small cymbals produce a high-pitched sustained sound when struck together. For the best sound, hold them perpendicular to each other and strike only the edges, rather than the entire circumference, of the cymbals together.

gankogui (gahn-KOH-gwee)   This double-bell originates in Ghana, West Africa, and is held from the top and played with a small stick.

gong   This instrument originated in Asia and is one of the world's oldest bells. The large, flat surface produces a complex, low-pitched tone when struck with a mallet. Gongs come in variety of sizes and add an exotic element to the music.

pagoda bells (pah-GOH-dah), also called **rotary bells**, or **Tibetan bells** These small brass bells are connected with a string and tuned to almost the same pitch. They produce a high-pitched chorused effect when struck together. One of the bells may be swung around in a circle after it is struck to modulate the sound and add vibrato.

sleigh bells   Sleigh bells are sets of small round bells that produce a shimmer effect when shaken. They often come mounted on sticks, which makes them easy to play.

tambourine (tam-boh-REEN)   A frame drum with jingles set into the shell, the tambourine comes with or without heads, and although it is technically a drum, the primary sound of the instrument comes from the metal jingles (cymbals) that line its shell. The tambourine may also fall under the rattle group because of the way it is played.

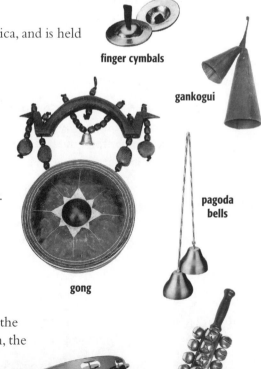

agogo

cowbell

finger cymbals

gankogui

pagoda bells

gong

tambourine

sleigh bells

triangle   The triangle is a metal bar formed into a triangle shape and open at one corner. It is played by suspending it from the index finger or on a string and striking the lower portion with a small metal beater.

Note: Never play any of the other instruments with a triangle beater. It is made of very hard metal and could cause damage.

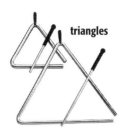
triangles

wind chimes   Wind chimes are small, graduated metal bars that produce a complex series of high-pitched tones. A set will often come with mounting brackets so they can be attached to a cymbal stand for easy access.

windchimes

 PITCHED PERCUSSION

Percussion Tubes

Boomwhackers® Percussion Tubes (Boomwhackers®)   The whacky invention of my friend Craig Ramsell, these multi-colored plastic tubes have become a favorite among music educators and drum circle facilitators all over the world. They are lightweight, durable, and available in a range of pitches and colors. Find out more at WhackyMusic.com.

Joia Tubes (JOY-yah)   Rick Kramer invented these tuned PVC tubes. They are played with soft paddles and produce a sound that is a cross between a pop-gun sound and a "thwack!" They may also be played individually. Find out more at Joia.com.

boomwhackers®

Barred Instruments

xylophone   With its roots in Africa, the xylophone is one of the oldest pitched-percussion instruments. It features graduated wooden bars that are tuned to specific pitches.

metallophone   This educational instrument is modeled after the *gamelons* of Bali and features graduated metal bars that are tuned to specific pitches. It is similar to the vibraphone, the professional version.

glockenspiel (GLOH-ken-shpeel), or **orchestra bells**   The glockenspiel features small graduated metal bars that are tuned to specific pitches (higher than the notes of a metallophone). It is played with hard rubber or wooden mallets.

joia tubes

A group of barred "Orff instruments." To find out more about Orff instruments, visit Peripole.com.

Plucked Instruments

kalimba (kah-LIM-bah), also called **mbira** (em-BEER-ah), or **thumb piano**   Rooted in Africa, the mbira, or thumb piano, is a small wood or gourd resonation chamber fitted with metal "keys" that are tuned to specific pitches. The keys are played with the tips of the fingers and thumbs.

Embira (em-BEER-ah)   The Embira is an electric thumb piano, created by Lucinda Ellison. It features a hardwood body and electric output for use with amplifiers or recording devices.

To find out more about thumb pianos, visit HarmonicJourney.com.

embira

BODY PERCUSSION

clap   This is how we let people know that we like what they did! We use it to reinforce the backbeat of a song and to play pat-a-cake with our friends. We can make it bright and high by holding our hands flat or clapping with the fingers into the palm, and we can make it sound dark and low by cupping the hands. Claps are a little lower in pitch than snaps are and can be associated with the shakers, rattles and scrapers when substituting body percussion for instruments.

pat   Your lap may disappear when you stand up, but you can still pat your thighs. We do this when we want someone to sit in our lap or when we're just following along with the beat when listening to music. We can pat our legs faster than clapping or snapping because it's a simple movement that uses both hands. Patting provides a lower pitch than clapping and can be associated with the wood sounds when substituting for instruments.

snap   This simple two-fingered technique produces a short, high-pitched sound and has been likened to the sound of raindrops. It's the highest-pitched body percussion sound and can be associated with the metal sounds when substituting for instruments.

stamp, or **stomp**   We do this when we're really excited, or sometimes when we're angry, and we want everyone to know. "One, two, three, four, we are stamping on the floor!" Stomping is a good way to feel a steady beat because it uses large body movements. It creates the lowest body percussion sound and can be associated with the drums when substituting for instruments.

In addition to the four standard body percussion techniques described above, two additional techniques from musician/dancer Keith Terry add even more possibilities:

   chest   Patting the upper chest.

   tush   Patting the back of the upper leg.

To learn more about Keith Terry's body music techniques (innovative ways to make music with your body), visit his website, Crosspulse.com.

Vocal Percussion

Common uses of vocal sounds in a drum circle setting include names of things such as people or instruments, short phrases, chants, and songs. In the Kodály (koh-DYE) approach to music education (named after Zoltan Kodály, 1882–1967), participants use various sounds, such as *Ti*, *Ta*, and *Toe* to represent notes of different durations. See page 95 for more information.

Appendix B

Instrument Quick Reference Chart

The following chart provides basic characteristics of the primary instruments. Use it to quickly find instruments that have common features such as all the low-volume instruments or those that are easy to play. The qualities I have identified are generalizations based on typical playing style; individual experiences may vary. **Volume**, **size**, and **pitch** values are relative to the other instruments in the group. **Technique** refers to the learning curve for standard techniques, not accessibility; for example, the riq is easy to pick up and hit, but it takes time to learn how to play it in the traditional manner. **Group** is used to indicate the types of participants for which an instrument is typically well-suited, although the same instrument may also work for other groups as well.

Category	Instrument	Volume Low	Volume Medium	Volume High	Size Small	Size Medium	Size Large	Pitch Low	Pitch Medium	Pitch High	Technique Easy	Technique Moderate	Technique Advanced	Timbre Dark	Timbre Medium	Timbre Bright	Group General	Group Children	Group Special Needs
Bass Drums	Dundun			•			•	•	•			•		•			•	•	
Bass Drums	Harmony	•				•			•		•			•				•	•
Bass Drums	Surdo		•				•	•			•			•			•		•
Hand Drums	Ashiko		•				•		•				•		•		•		
Hand Drums	Bongo		•			•				•			•		•		•		
Hand Drums	Cajon		•			•			•			•			•		•		
Hand Drums	Conga		•				•		•				•		•		•		
Hand Drums	Doumbek		•			•				•			•		•		•		
Hand Drums	Jembe			•			•	•	•	•			•		•		•		
Hand Drums	Sienta Conga		•				•		•			•			•		•	•	•
Hand Drums	Sienta Jembe			•			•	•	•	•		•			•		•	•	•
Frame Drums	Bendir	•				•		•				•		•			•		
Frame Drums	Bodhran	•				•		•					•	•			•		•
Frame Drums	Hand Drum	•			•	•		•	•	•	•				•		•	•	•
Frame Drums	Tamborim			•	•					•			•		•		•		
Frame Drums	Tar	•				•				•		•			•			•	•
Rattles	Axatse		•		•					•	•				•			•	•
Rattles	Cabasa	•			•					•		•			•		•		•
Rattles	Caxixi		•		•					•	•				•			•	•
Rattles	Maracas	•			•					•	•				•			•	•
Rattles	Pod Rattle		•		•					•	•				•		•	•	•
Rattles	Puili sticks		•			•			•	•				•			•	•	
Rattles	Shékere			•		•				•		•			•		•		
Shakers	Egg	•			•					•	•				•			•	•
Shakers	Tube	•			•				•			•			•		•		
Scrapers	Frogs/crickets	•			•				•	•	•				•			•	•
Scrapers	Guiro		•		•				•			•			•		•		
Scrapers	Reco-Reco		•		•				•						•		•		

	Instrument	Volume			Size			Pitch			Technique			Timbre			Group		
		Low	Medium	High	Small	Medium	Large	Low	Medium	High	Easy	Moderate	Advanced	Dark	Medium	Bright	General	Children	Special Needs
Bells	Agogo		•		•				•			•				•	•	•	
	Cowbell			•	•				•	•	•					•	•	•	•
	Finger Cymbals	•			•					•	•					•		•	
	Gankogui		•		•				•		•				•		•		
	Gong		•		•	•			•		•				•		•		
	Rotary Bells		•		•					•	•					•	•	•	
	Sleigh Bells		•		•					•	•					•		•	•
	Triangle		•		•					•	•	•				•	•	•	
	Wind Chimes	•				•				•	•					•	•		•
Wood	Clapper Sticks		•			•				•	•				•		•	•	•
	Clave			•	•					•	•	•			•		•		
	Slit Drum	•			•	•			•		•			•			•	•	•
	Temple Blocks		•		•				•		•					•	•	•	•
	Woodblock			•	•					•	•					•	•	•	•
Pitched	Boomwhackers®		•			•		•	•		•					•	•	•	•
	Joia Tubes		•				•	•	•			•				•	•	•	•
	Barred	•	•		•	•	•	•	•	•		•	•	•	•	•	•	•	•
	Kalimba/ Embira	•			•				•	•		•	•		•		•		

Are there other instruments that are used in drum circles?

Of course! Instruments such as didjeridoos,[4] flutes, found sounds (pots, pans, buckets, boxes, etc.), homemade instruments, and drumsets are often used, but the instruments listed above are the most common and best suited for groups of all kinds.

Building an Instrument Kit

When it comes to drums circles, many possible combinations of instruments can be used, and factors such as size, volume and playability need to be considered when putting together a kit. It's always best to offer a wide variety of instruments from each of the four main timbre groups (drums, wood sounds, shakers and bells). This way the instruments represent the vast array of sounds that are available, supporting the idea that variety is a good thing. This isn't to say that every drum circle must be made up of different types of instruments. I've experienced wonderful music that was created by just using frame drums (hand drums), body percussion, and percussion tubes. But as a general rule, the more options you can provide for your participants, the richer their experience will be.

If you are going to be supplying instruments for the participants, I recommend starting off with 50% drums, 20% shakers/rattles, 20% wood sounds, and 10% bells. These proportions create a nice balance between the various timbres while supplying your participants with a wide variety of instruments. The following charts provide examples of different types of kits for various applications. Of course, your budget and personal preferences will also determine how you put together your own kit, but these examples will give you a place to start and some ideas to build upon.

Sample Kits

Starter Kit: Low cost and easy to transport.

Drums	Shakers	Wood	Metal	Pitched
(15) frame (hand) drums (3 sets)	(2) axatse/maracas	(2) clapper sticks	(1) agogo bell	(5) sets pentatonic Boomwhackers® Percussion Tubes (6 per set)
(2) jembes or ashikos	(2) caxixi	(6) tone (two-tone) blocks	(1) tambourine	
(3) Sienta congas	(6) shakers	(2) woodblocks	(2) triangles	

Full Kit (add to starter kit): Great for all kinds of groups.

Drums	Shakers/Scrapers	Wood	Metal	Pitched
(4) jembe/ashikos	(2) cabasa (afuche)	(1) clave (pair)	(1) gankogui	(1) 5-note bass set Joia Tubes
(2) bass drums	(2) guiro/reco-reco	(4) wooden frogs	(1) pair pagoda bells	
(2) bongos	(1) shékere		(2) cowbells	(1) 9-note pentatonic set Joia Tubes
(2) congas				

Children's Kit: Medium-volume and easy-to-play instruments.

Drums	Shakers	Wood	Metal	Pitched
(3) Harmony floor drums (1 set)	(2) axatse	(4) frogs/crickets	(2) agogo bells	(4) sets Boomwhackers® Percussion Tubes
(15) Rainbow hand drums (3 sets)	(3) caxixi	(2) clapper sticks	(1) gankogui	
(3) Sienta congas	(1) guiro	(1) slit drum	(1) pair pagoda bells	
(2) Sienta jembes	(4) shakers	(2) tone (two-tone) blocks	(1) tambourine	

Items to include with any kit:

(10) circle mallets for frame drums

(12) circle sticks for wood sounds

(4) pairs of Vic Firth Handtones for hand drums

(6) pairs of Hand Drumming Gloves

(2) dundun sticks

(4) bags for percussion instruments and sticks

(1) rolling case

Rhythm Basics

Counting Rhythm

If you're not familiar with reading and counting music, take a couple of moments to review this exercise. Most of the examples in this book are based on simple rhythms that use both *downbeats* (pulse) and *upbeats* (notes between the downbeats). Also known as steady beat and divided beat.

Simple pulse counting

Beat	1	2	3	4	1	2	3	4
Step	right	left	right	left	right	left	right	left
Say	"One"	"Two"	"Three"	"Four"	"One"	"Two"	"Three"	"Four"

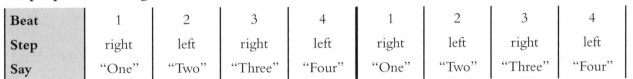

Qtr Note

1   2   3   4   1   2   3   4

Adding upbeats to the pulse

Beat	1	+	2	+	3	+	4	+
Clap		clap		clap		clap		clap
Step	right		left		right		left	
Say	"One"	"and"	"Two"	"and"	"Three"	"and"	"Four"	"and"

Eighth Note

1 + 2 + 3 + 4 + 1 + 2 + 3 + 4 +

As previously mentioned, the Kodály approach to music education uses various vocal sounds such as *Ti*, *Ta*, and *Toe* to represent notes of different durations.

Ti = *Eighth note* **1/2 beat** • Ta = *Quarter note* **1 full beat** • Toe = *Half note* **2 full beats**

1	+	2	+	3	+	4	+	1	+	2	+	3	+	4	+
Ta		Ta		Ti	Ti	Ta		Ti	Ti	Ta		Toe			

Kodály

Ta   Ta   Ti Ti Ta   Ti Ti Ta   Toe

To practice the above example,

- step to the pulse (1 right, 2 left, etc.);
- pat your legs twice as fast as your steps (1 + 2 + 3 + 4 +, etc.);
- say the vocal sounds while you keep stepping and patting.

To learn more about the Kodály approach, visit http://oake.org/ or http://www.kodaly-inst.hu/.

Building a Group Vocal Groove

Here's an example of how you might build a vocal groove by chanting the names of some instruments.

1	+	2	+	3	+	4	+
Tri-		an-	gle	Tri-		an-	gle
Sha-	ker	Sha-	ker	Sha-	ker	Shake	
Wood-	block			Wood-	block		
Drum				Drum		Drum	

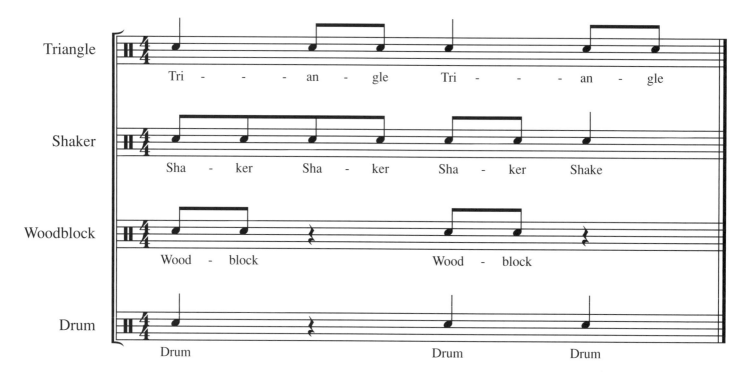

Process

1. Chant the triangle line in rhythm. Repeat several times and invite everyone to join you.

2. Repeat step 1 for the other three lines.

3. With the group chanting the DRUM line, cue half to continue, stop the other half and have them chant the SHAKER line.

4. Cue half of the DRUM group to change to the TRIANGLE line.

5. Cue half of the SHAKER group to change to the WOODBLOCK line.

6. Pause and have each group switch to the part of the group to their left (or right).

Extension

- Have the group chant each line in order (16 beats total).

- Divide the group into four equal sections and have them chant the 16-beat phrase in canon.

- Substitute body percussion: snap=triangle, pat=shaker, clap=woodblock, stamp=drum

- Transfer the lines to their corresponding instruments.

I often have groups move to vocal percussion at some point during an event to help them connect with their "original instrument" and feel the rhythms from the inside out. Vocal percussion jams can bring out the creativity in the group because everyone can already "play" these sounds, and there aren't the technical barriers associated with learning how to play instruments.

Appendix E

Table of DCMI Symbols

(Drum Circle Music Iconography)

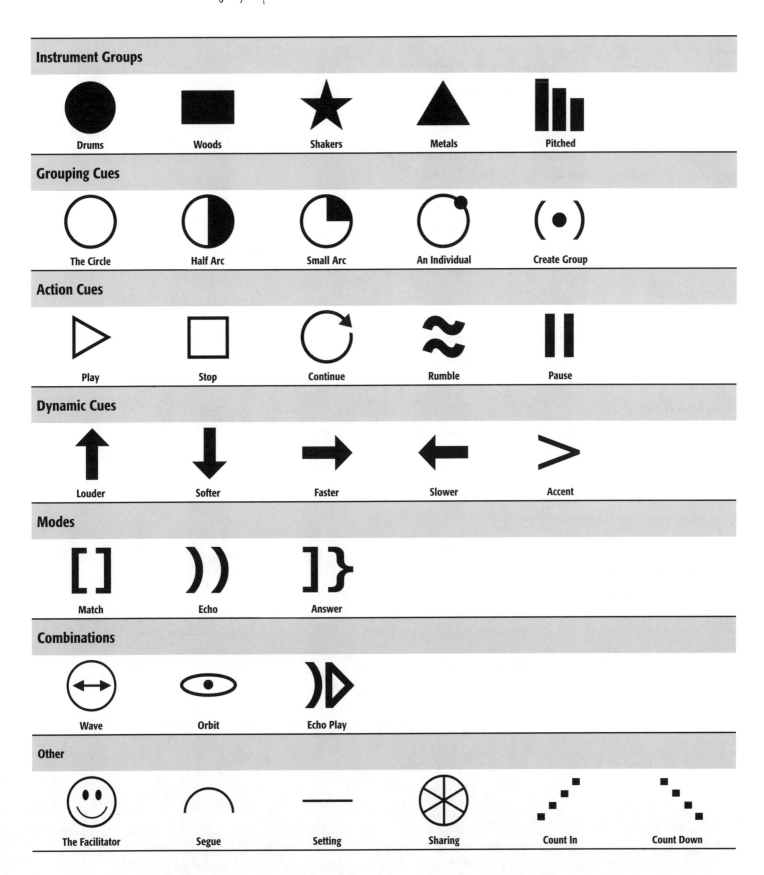

Instrument Groups

| Drums | Woods | Shakers | Metals | Pitched |

Grouping Cues

| The Circle | Half Arc | Small Arc | An Individual | Create Group |

Action Cues

| Play | Stop | Continue | Rumble | Pause |

Dynamic Cues

| Louder | Softer | Faster | Slower | Accent |

Modes

| Match | Echo | Answer |

Combinations

| Wave | Orbit | Echo Play |

Other

| The Facilitator | Segue | Setting | Sharing | Count In | Count Down |

Appendix F

DCM Training Programs

Drum Circle Music certification training programs are designed around Kalani's innovative and successful facilitation techniques and strategies. They provide participants with a dynamic learning environment that pulsates with energy, information and fun!

An abundance of useful activities and drum circle games are presented in a setting of exploration and creative learning. Instructor and peer feedback help each participant gain valuable insights into their potential and empower them to grow on many levels.

The network of DCM facilitators provides you with ongoing support as you develop your skills in your community. Participants are encouraged to share success stories, activities, games and strategies with other DCM facilitators through e-mail lists and the DCM website.

Benefits of Participation

- Play and learn about instruments that are used in drum circles.
- Develop facilitation techniques, strategies and presentation skills.
- Learn how to use the drum circle format in your profession.
- Gain valuable business tools, resources and feedback.
- Facilitate a community-style drum circle.
- Increase your presentation, leadership and "followership" skills.
- Improve your sense of rhythm and your drumming techniques.
- Learn how to plan, organize, promote and present a rhythm-based event.

Who Should Attend?

- Music teachers and school teachers
- Therapists and social workers
- Health care providers
- Recreation activity directors
- Drum circle facilitators
- Anyone who loves music and people

Professional Standards

If you are a music educator or music therapist, you will find that Drum Circle Music supports the goals and standards of your profession and provides useful activities that can easily be incorporated into your work. If you are new to drum circles or even to music, DCM provides you with everything you need to facilitate group music making with confidence. If you are an experienced drum circle facilitator, you will find many valuable resources that will help you take your art to the next level and beyond.

Continuing Education Credits

Course credits are available for music educators, music therapists, counselors and other professionals. See the Drum Circle Music website for details (DrumCircleMusic.com).

Our Mission

The mission of Kalani Music is to develop relevant and valuable resources and technologies, as well as professional development opportunities, that meet or exceed the current professional standards of music educators, music therapists and others in related professions. We are committed to the growth and success of each participant.

The National Standards for Music Education

Performing, creating, and responding to music are the fundamental music processes in which humans engage. Students, particularly those in grades K–4, learn by doing. Singing, playing instruments, moving to music, and creating music enables them to acquire musical skills and knowledge that can be developed in no other way. Learning to read and notate music gives them a skill with which to explore music independently and with others. Listening to, analyzing, and evaluating music are important building blocks of musical learning. Furthermore, to participate fully in a diverse, global society, students must understand their own historical and cultural heritage and that of others within their communities and beyond. Because music is a basic expression of human culture, every student should have access to a balanced, comprehensive, and sequential program of study in music.

Standards

1. Singing, alone and with others, a varied repertoire of music.

2. Performing on instruments, alone and with others, a varied repertoire of music.

3. Improvising melodies, variations, and accompaniments.

4. Composing and arranging music within specified guidelines.

5. Reading and notating music.

6. Listening to, analyzing, and describing music.

7. Evaluating music and music performances.

8. Understanding relationships between music, the other arts, and disciplines outside the arts.

9. Understanding music in relation to history and culture.

Source: From *National Standards for Arts Education*. Copyright © 1994 by Music Educators National Conference (MENC). Used by permission. The complete National Arts Standards and additional materials relating to the Standards are available from MENC—The National Association for Music Education, 1806 Robert Fulton Drive, Reston, VA 20191.

Glossary

canon: Literally meaning "rule," a system in which one musical line is imitated by all others after a specific amount of time (or beats) has passed. One popular type of canon is the *round*: "Row, Row, Row Your Boat" is an example of a round.

ceremony: A formal act or series of acts as prescribed by ritual, protocol, or convention.

circle: (1) A group of persons sharing a common interest (2) A musical gathering.

community: (1) An interacting population of various kinds of individuals. (2) Joint ownership or participation.

cooperate: To associate with another or others for mutual benefit.

drummer: One who plays a drum. Sometimes used figuratively in phrases denoting unconventional thought or action, as in, "marching to the beat of a different drummer."

entrain: (1) To travel at the same speed, as aboard a train. (2) To align in rhythm.

facilitator: One who helps others reach their goals or makes something easier to achieve.

group: (1) (noun) A number of people sharing something in common. (2) (verb) To define specific members of the circle.

haiku: A Japanese poetry form, usually in three lines with syllables numbering 5–7–5.

Jamnasium: A place for musical exploration, group activities and creative expression.

iconography: The set of symbols or images used in a particular field of activity, recognized as having a particular meaning.

Kodály: A pedagogical approach to music education (created by Zoltan Kodály) with an emphasis on singing and teaching rhythm through a system of specific vocalizations.

labyrinth: A place, often contained within a circle, that features a single path moving from edge to center along a series of "circuits." They are used by many as a tool for personal, psychological and spiritual transformation.

listen: (1) To hear something with thoughtful attention. (2) To be alert in order to catch an unexpected sound.

mandala: An integrated structure organized around a unifying center. The word is Sanskrit and may be loosely translated as "circle." A labyrinth is a type of mandala.

music: (1) The science or art of ordering tones or sounds in succession, in combination, and in temporal relationships, in order to produce a composition having unity and continuity. (2) An agreeable sound.

orbit: Moving around the circumference of the circle, either sonically or physically.

Orff-Schulwerk: A pedagogical approach to music and movement education that incorporates an intuitive and holistic learning process.

recreation: (1) Refreshment of strength and spirits after work. (2) Restoration to health.

resting: Active listening while creating space in the music by not playing.

rhythm: (1) An ordered recurrent alteration of strong and weak elements in the flow of sound. (2) The aspect of music comprising all the elements that relate to forward movement through time.

riding: Playing an identifiable pattern that repeats.

riffing: (1) Soloing. (2) Playing in an improvisatory manner.

ritual: (1) The established form for a ceremony. (2) To fit together.

rolling: Playing with alternating and balanced movements to produce a stream of notes.

segue: (1) A smooth transition from one state to another. (2) A musical bridge, used to connect settings.

setting: A unique activity or system within a drum circle program.

sharing: A time to reflect, share, and discuss thoughts and feelings.

sound scape: A freeform exploration of sound that focuses on aspects of music other than rhythm such as timbres, dynamics and pitch.

synergy: A mutually advantageous relationship of distinct elements through combined action.

system: A regularly interacting or independent group of items forming a unified whole.

Tashiko Fitness Drumming: A combination of techniques and activities created by Kalani that include drumming, physical exercise, and other practices beneficial to one's physical and mental health.

unity: (1) A totality of related parts. (2) An entity that is complex or systematically whole.

Bibliography

Arrien, Angeles. *The Four-Fold Way: Walking the Paths of the Warrior, Teacher, Healer and Visionary*. San Francisco: Harper SanFracisco, 1993.

Baldwin, Christina. *Calling the Circle: The First and Future Culture*. New York: Bantam Books, 1998.

Beachner, Lynne, and Anola Pickett. *Multiple Intelligences and Positive Life Habits.: 174 Activities for Applying Them in Your Classroom*. Thousand Oaks: Corwin Press, 2001.

Campbell, Joseph, with Bill Moyers. *The Power of Myth*. Edited by Betty Sue Flowers. New York: Doubleday, 1988.

Campbell, Linda, Bruce Campbell, and Dee Dickinson. *Teaching and Learning Through Multiple Intelligences*. Needham Heights: Allyn & Bacon, 1996.

Gardner, Howard. *Frames of Mind: The Theory of Multiple Intelligences*. New York: Basic Books, 1983.

Gaynor, Mitchell L. *The Healing Power of Sound: Recovery from Life-Threatening Illness Using Sound, Voice, and Music*. Boston: Shambhala Publications, 1999.

Gibbs, Jeanne. *Tribes: A New Way of Learning and Being Together*. Sausalito: Center Source Systems, LLC, 2001.

Gibson, Leslie Ann. *The Woman's Book of Positive Quotations*. Minneapolis: Fairview Press, 2002.

Goodkin, Doug. *Play, Sing, & Dance: An Introduction to Orff Schulwerk*. New York: Schott, 2002.

Goodkin, Doug. *Sound Ideas: Activities for the Percussion Circle*. Miami: Warner Bros., 2002.

Hawkins, Holly Blue. *The Heart of the Circle: A Guide to Drumming*. Freedom: Crossing Press, 1999.

Hull, Arthur. *Drum Circle Spirit: Facilitating Human Potential Through Rhythm*. Tempe: White Cliffs Media, 1998.

Merriam-Webster's Collegiate Dictionary, Tenth Edition. Merriam-Webster, Inc., 2002

O'Connor, Joseph, and John Seymour. *Introducing Neuro-Linguistic Programming: Psychological Skills for Understanding and Influencing People*. Mandala 1990, Aquarian Press 1993

Quotable Quotes. Reader's Digest, 1997.

Stevens, Christine. *The Art and Heart of Drum Circles*. Milwaukee: Hal Leonard, 2003.

(Footnotes)

[1] See the game "Stitch in Time" in the *Amazing Jamnasium*.

[2] See page 99 for detailed descriptions of the National Standards for Music Education.

[3] See "Getting to Know You" on page 56.

[4] A **didjeridoo** (dih-jeh-ree-DOO), also called "didj" for short, is an ancient Australian "trumpet" made from a eucalyptus branch that has been hollowed out by termites, painted, and fitted with a wax mouth piece.

Kalani Signature Series Recreational Drumming Accessories

Handtone–A high-density plastic implement covered with open cell neoprene on one side. Provides an alternative to playing with the hands, and keeps drums safe and sounding good. Great for music therapy applications and contemporary music settings.

Circle Sticks–Produce excellent sound on small hand-held percussion instruments including woodblock, cowbell, tone block, frame drum, and more. Easy to hold and control. Won't damage instruments like larger sticks. Packs of 12 include 3 each of red, blue, green, and yellow sticks.

Hand-Drumming Gloves–Provide hand protection while producing a musically-pleasing result. Exposed fingertips produce crisp slap tones while padded palms produce open and bass tones. Gives drummers confidence while keeping them safe. Designed for recreational drummers, teachers, music therapists, and drum-circle facilitators. Perfect for all types of hand drums. Available in various sizes.

Dundun Stick–An authentic stick for full dynamic range without added weight. Designed for dundun, taiko drums, and any other bass drums with cowhide or similar heads. Beveled shaft makes it easy to hold and use. Available in ash. Sold singly.

Circle Mallet 1–A medium-soft rubber mallet that is perfect for 8-inch to 12-inch frame drums. Works well on barred instruments and other drums. Maple shaft. Sold singly.

Circle Mallet 2–A soft rubber mallet for frame drums that are 12 inches or larger. Works well on barred instruments and other drums. Maple shaft. Sold singly.

Circle Mallet 3–A medium-soft rubber mallet covered with fleece. Perfect for soft playing on 8-inch to 12-inch frame drums. Helps keep the volume down and brings out the full tone of the drum. Maple shaft. Sold singly.

Circle Mallet 4–A soft rubber mallet covered with fleece. For soft playing on frame drums that are 12 inches or larger. Helps keep the volume down while producing a soft, melodic tone. Maple shaft. Sold singly.

The Kalani Drum Circle Series is designed to keep your participants safe and sounding their best. Everyone can drum to their heart's content without having to worry about hurting their hands or damaging expensive drums or small percussion instruments. These are the right tools for recreational drummers, kids, and people with special needs. Visit vicfirth.com for a dealer near you.

More great drum books from Kalani and Alfred Publishing...

All about Jembe, Congas & Bongos

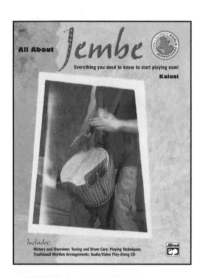

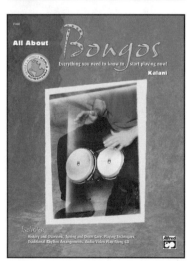

This series of books, with enhanced CDs, provides everything students need to start playing the jembe, bongos and congas. Contents include history and background, drum types and anatomy, tuning up, playing positions and techniques, hand and rhythm exercises, practice tips, rhythm patterns (both traditional and contemporary), performance ensembles, and drum care including how to replace both traditional and contemporary-style heads. The enhanced CD may be played as an audio CD or used with a PC or Mac to show video clips of all the techniques and rhythms in the book.

 Alfred Publishing Co., Inc.